Early Aviation in North Wales

EARLY AVIATION
in
NORTH WALES

Roy Sloan

GWASG CARREG GWALCH

*ISBN: 0-86381-119-1
Front cover by Anne Lloyd Morris*

*First published on 1st May, 1989
by Gwasg Carreg Gwalch, Capel Garmon,
Llanrwst, Gwynedd, Wales.
Tel: 06902 261*

CONTENTS

THE AUTHOR

The author was born at Bangor in 1945 and spent his formative years on his grandparents farm in Anglesey. Educated at Beaumaris Grammar School, he joined the local Air Training Corps squadron, which gave him his first taste of flying and awakened a lifelong interest in aviation.

After leaving school he moved to London, where he worked for the Ministry of Aviation. Subsequently he has been employed by the Ministry of Defence and the Royal Air Force and at present is the Careers Librarian at the University College of North Wales, Bangor.

Apart from aviation, his other interests include mountaineering, photography and music.

He has contributed articles to a number of magazines and taken part in radio programmes on Welsh aviation but this is his first book.

INTRODUCTION AND ACKNOWLEDGEMENTS

Although possessing a lifelong interest in aviation my knowledge of events and developments in Gwynedd was always sketchy in the extreme, particularly the early days of flying. I did not know when the first flight in North Wales took place, for example, or what effect the First World War had on aviation in the area. The major facts of aviation history, on a national and international basis were known to me, but of what had taken place 'on the doorstep' so to speak, I was totally ignorant.

Then, during the early part of 1981, whilst trying to gather some information for a friend on a flying accident which had taken place in Snowdonia, I found myself thinking a great deal about local aviation and I realised how scant my knowledge was.

So, I decided to remedy this deficiency by finding answers to some of the questions I was asking myself. I began to visit archives and museums. At first my research was rather perfunctory and not very serious but after a short while, when I discovered how few printed sources were available and how much original work would have to be done from primary sources I became aware that a most interesting challenge was presenting itself. In no time at all I found myself engaged upon a research project which, although it seemed to have come about almost by accident, now fired me with enthusiasm and to which I devoted a great deal of time and energy.

The task I set myself was to compile a history of aviation in Gwynedd and North Wales from the earliest days of the pioneers to the present day activities of fast jets. This volume forms the first part of that history.

I have attempted to make the text as readable and lively

as possible, combining basic factual information with anecdotal material at every opportunity. This approach will, I hope, appeal to both aviation enthusiast and layman alike.

Although I have tried to be as rigorous as possible in checking and cross checking facts, errors are bound to occur in compiling a work of this kind but I hope that the inevitable mistakes are few in number.

During my research it has been my pleasure and privilege to come into contact with so many interesting and informative people either in person or by letter and I must express my heartfelt thanks and gratitude to them all for their generous help.

Special thanks must go to Tomos Roberts, archivist at the University College of North Wales, Bangor, whose friendly helpfulness and extensive personal knowledge of papers held within the archive makes the life of any researcher that much easier; the staff of Gwynedd Archives, including Gareth Haulfryn Williams, deputy archivist, Anne Venables and Christine Owen, who made the job of searching through the yellowing pages of old newspapers such a delight!

Also, Gwenith Parry and Mrs Vera Bradford at the Llangefni office of Gwynedd Archives. My thanks to them for their kindness and help and for making me so welcome during my numerous visits.

Other individuals whom I wish to thank include Mr Owen Rowlands, Mr O. J. Williams, both of Llanddona, plus many others from the same village; Mr William Hugh Jones of Llanfairynghornwy, Mr Robin Williams, Mynydd Mechell, Mr Owen Owens of Rhydwyn. Thanks also to the other inhabitants, too numerous to mention here, of Llanfairynghornwy, that most Welsh of Anglesey villages.

My thanks to the Pritchard family of Glanymor Isaf farm, Bangor, Mr F. Pritchard of Star, Gaerwen, Mrs Jean Williams of Talysarn, Dyffryn Nantlle, Dr D. Wright, Maths department, U.C.N.W., Mr O. G. Foulkes of Bodorgan, Anglesey, and Alderman Charles M. Jones of

Bala, with whom I spent a truly memorable afternoon listening to his reminiscences of R.N.A.S. Llangefni during the far off days of World War I.

I must express my gratitude also to Mr Neil Lewis for his much appreciated advice and friendly criticism of my manuscript. Without the benefit of his experience the end result would have been that much poorer.

Thanks also to the staff of the Royal Air Force Museum, Hendon, the Imperial War Museum and that vast treasure house of information, the Public Record Office.

There are many others also who have rendered assistance to me, either in small or large measure, in the preperation of this work. I am greatly indepted to them all.

For me researching the story of aviation in North Wales has provided a wealth of interest which I did not think possible when I first embarked upon the venture. I can only hope that the reader will also find something of interest in the pages that follow.

Roy Sloan, Brynsiencyn,
February 1988.

Chapter 1

EARLY BALLOON FLIGHTS

The first aerial craft seen in the skies of Gwynedd was a balloon in October 1812. It was flown by James Sadler, an adventurous aeronaut of the period, whilst attempting the first crossing of the Irish Sea by air.

The son of an Oxford pastrycook, Sadler possessed great ambition and had already undertaken a number of exciting and hazardous flights. Though nearly sixty years old at the time of this particular flight his vigour and determination remained undiminished by age.

Full of enthusiasm, he constructed a new balloon for the purpose, with a diameter of 55 feet, 87,000 cubic feet gas capacity and carrying over half a ton of ballast.

On October 1st, according to the *North Wales Gazette*, "Mr. Sadler ascended from the Belvedere Grounds, Dublin about one o'clock, with the wind at south west, and in a gradual and majestic style left the shores of Ireland amidst the huzzas of an incredible number of spectators."

After only a few minutes in the air he noticed that gas was leaking through a defect in the envelope at a point out of reach, but, with commendable initiative, he quickly tied some cord across the ropes by which the basket was suspended and climbed up this improvised ladder to repair the leak with his own neckerchief. Borne along by a favourable wind Sadler eventually reached the Isle of Man where he decided to discharge ballast in order to climb. As the balloon ascended it encountered a northerly wind, which then took it to Anglesey.

Continuing across the island, and with the mainland coast approaching, Sadler, ambitious as ever, decided to carry on and make for Liverpool. Had he landed at this point, the flight would have been regarded as a great success, but to try and reach Liverpool was, frankly, over-ambitious. Sadler hoped to carry out this plan by descending and thereby coming under the influence once again of the south westerly winds which had been so favourable during the early part of the flight. By 4.30 p.m. he reached the Great Orme, where, unfortunately, a setback occurred: due to the contrariness of the air currents, the wind unexpectedly veered to the south forcing the balloon out to sea.

Sadler had always maintained that a balloonist should be able to control the direction of his craft by ascending or descending to locate the most favourable winds, and that is exactly what he did, but to no avail.

With dusk approaching and the balloon being blown relentlessly out to sea he decided to come down near two ships. However, they did not see him, and so he then re-ascended. After a while Sadler saw another ship, and descended once more. Luckily this time the vessel, a Manx fishing boat, had seen the balloon and came to the rescue. It was accomplished in a most unusual manner when the captain ran his ship's bowsprit through the balloon! The flight had lasted six hours, and Sadler estimated that he travelled 43 miles over land and 237 miles over water. His attempt would have succeeded had Sadler's undoubted skill in handling the balloon not led to over-confidence. Despite his navigational abilities, he remained essentially, like all balloonists, at the mercy of the wind.

The next attempt at the Irish Sea crossing was made in 1817 by another Sadler, James's 21 year old son, Windham, to whom James had imparted all his ballooning skills.

During July father and son were in Dublin making preparations for the flight. On the 22nd conditions were ideal with fine weather and a favourable wind. Windham left from the Portobello Barracks, alone, at 2.20 p.m. and headed gently out over the sea. Five hours later, after a straightforward flight at an average speed of 13 m.p.h., Sadler's balloon was approaching Anglesey, and came down eventually at Pen y Bryn farm, near Holyhead (the actual site has long since disappeared under Holyhead's urban growth).

A correspondent of the *North Wales Gazette* gives this account of events, — "The inhabitants of this neighbourhood have witnessed this evening a very novel sight and probably the only one of its kind ever seen in this part of the Empire. A balloon was observed at a great height from different parts of the parish and an immense concourse of men, women and children soon followed the course which it took and at the distance of about 3 miles from this town, they were gratified with the sight of it safely landed, and the aeronaut Mr. Sadler junior handed out of the car unhurt and in good spirits; his grappling iron for some time was incapable of stopping the progress of the car and balloon, but at length, with the assistance of some men who were on the spot, it was brought to an anchor ... Mr. Sadler arrived at Holyhead in a chaise, about eight o'clock; the car and all the apparatus were conveyed to Spencers Hotel, uninjured, by a number of seamen who had repaired to the spot to witness the descent — Holyhead, Tuesday Evening July 22nd 1817."

The Irish Sea crossing had at last been achieved. Doubtless James Sadler must have been delighted at his son's success, particularly the ease with which Windham seemed to have attained his goal. Of course luck played an important part, as it always does in such adventures, but the Sadlers were skilful balloonists and deserved their success.

Some years later, during the middle of the century, a local aristocrat, Lord Newborough of Glynllifon, was taking an interest in ballooning. It seems that he enjoyed dabbling in things mechanical, balloons included, and with far more money and time than most, indulged himself thoroughly. A most graphic piece of documentation concerning these activities is the following letter, written from Llanerchymedd, Anglesey, where one of the unmanned balloons came down, probably due to a gas leak:

"Ty Croes,
Llanerchymedd,
11th September, 1850.

My Lord,

I beg to appraise your Lordship that your Lordships Balloon alighted here a quarter before seven last night in a meadow belonging to this farm a distance from Glyn of about 28 miles, the part of this farm where it alighted is in the Parish of Llechcynfarwy.

The Balloon is a little torn and a strip rent from top to bottom and the rent appeared like a string to it, to them who first observed it coming down. Some of the children observed it when it was no larger than a bird. The Balloon descended in a frightful topsiturvy manner, terrifying the spectators awfully, the cattle that grazed in the meadow were bewildered in terror they did not know where to go far enough from the frightful object, they bellowed awfully.

The reapers who were in the field adjacent were much afrighted and did not know to what to ascribe this strange phenomenon and some of the strongest nerved of them advanced fearfully towards the spot where this monster then laid, with light steps and agitated breath.

The Balloon is here safe and will be sent according to your Lordships directions.

I am
my Lord
your Lordships
most humble servant
Thomas Griffith."

The first balloon seen in the region during this century was in February 1910 when, over 90 years after Windham Sadler's flight, another crossing of the Irish Sea was made by J. Dunville and C. Pollock. Their attempt in January had been foiled when the balloon, named "Banshee", was caught by a gust of wind during starting preparations and its envelope badly torn. After some weeks delay, while repairs were carried out, everything was ready and on February 15th the pair took off at 10.00 a.m. from Dublin.

The flight went well and by 12.30 p.m. they reached South Stack lighthouse. With the sea crossing safely behind them, they proceeded to fly along the North Wales coast towards Chester, succeeding in following the path which James Sadler had sought in vain to follow nearly a century previously.

Eventually Pollock became a balloon instructor with the newly formed Royal Naval Air Service. One of his pupils was a young officer by the name of T. B. Williams, who later spent much time in the air over Anglesey and the Irish Sea as an R. N. A. S. airship pilot on anti-submarine patrol.

Williams wrote of his mentor, "He was a genius at judging the alteration in wind direction at various heights, and often named the very area we would reach on a balloon journey," plainly a very desirable quality in any balloonist, and which explains why Pollock's Irish Sea flight was so successful.

No more flights occurred until 1921 when competitors in the International Gordon Bennett Balloon Race found themselves heading for North Wales. The race had started from Brussels on Sunday, September 18th, and by the following Tuesday morning two balloons reached Gwynedd.

One, belonging to a Belgian team made a rough landing near Rhydymain, six miles from Dolgellau, causing slight injuries to its occupants. The other, with two Americans, Ralph Upson and C. G. Andrews, on board, came down three miles from Aberdaron, on the Llŷn Peninsula. The pair had almost made it to Ireland, but as they approached the coast the wind dropped and completely becalmed them. Some hours were spent in a fruitless attempt to land until, eventually, the wind freshened, but from the wrong direction, much to the Americans disgust, as they were blown back across the Irish Sea.

In fact they tied for second place with a British competitor who descended at Fishguard — both achieved flights of 420 miles. The race was won that year by a Swiss balloonist, with a 470 mile flight to Lambay Island, near Dublin.

Chapter 2

EXHIBITION FLIGHTS

During the early years of aviation, aircraft, by virtue of their novelty, were always objects of intense public interest. The reality of flying was so exciting that any opportunity to witness flight would draw huge crowds. Many newly emergent aviators, and enterprising business men, aware of this interest and the commercial possibilities thereby opened up, organised competitions, meetings, and races at venues like Brooklands and Hendon which have become legends in aviation history. In addition, exhibition flights were also organised at many towns throughout the country which invariably proved immensely popular.

In Gwynedd the first show of this kind took place at Pwllheli. Some of the town elders and tradesmen had met in May 1911 to discuss forthcoming summer attractions, and, as much dissatisfaction was expressed at the previous year's lack of successful, crowd-pulling attractions, new ideas were called for. What better way to improve the situation, it was suggested. than by having a flying exhibition? Flight was the miracle of the age; North Wales was hardly touched by aviation, and a show of this kind would guarantee a large influx of visitors to the town; so the argument went.

The idea proved acceptable and after some enquiries Henry Astley, a young pilot of aristocratic background, was engaged to give exhibition flights during the Whitsun holiday, June 5th and 6th. The following advertisement then appeared in the local papers:

Newspaper advertisement for the flying exhibition at Pwllheli, 1911.

Astley was not amongst the first rank of aviators, but a promising, though inexperienced, beginner who had taken his Royal Aero Club certificate only a few months previously, in January. He flew a Birdling monoplane which was an imitation of the well-known Bleriot, made by Universal Aviation Ltd., a company owned by E. V. Sassoon (uncle of Victor and Siegfried) himself an enthusiastic pilot of Bleriot machines.

Prior to his appearance at Pwllheli, Astley had flown from Brooklands to Eton, and, being an old Etonian, made a landing on the playing fields of that famous school — the first to do so.

Whilst a cross country flight of this kind was possible a flight to North Wales remained impossible. The Birdling was dismantled, put into cases and sent to Pwllheli by rail. Astley himself arrived on Saturday June 3rd and took a room at the West End Hotel. He then inspected the area of ground between West End and South Beach, which the organising committee had suggested; but it was not to his liking, and he chose an alternative, the Recreation Ground — a bad choice as it later turned out. The monoplane meanwhile had been re-assembled and hangared.

It was fine and bright on Monday, as Pwllheli rapidly filled with people. The railway did good business carrying over four thousand passengers in to the town on cheap excursions. No more proof was needed of the astonishing crowd-pulling ability of the early aviators and their machines.

A sports meeting was in progress at the Recreation Ground but held little attraction as the *North Wales Chronicle* reported: "...when the grounds were thrown open on the Monday morning for the inspection of the monoplane by the public, a large crowd of people went there and were more engrossed in the aviation spectacle than in the programme of athletic sports which were in progress prior to the hour the aviator was timed to start on his machine. Considerable difficulty was experienced by Superintendent Jones and Sergeant Jones, who were in charge of the police in preventing the crowd surrounding the monoplane when it was moored opposite the grandstand. When the crowd were driven back on one side they surged round on the other, despite the fact that they were told the flight could not possibly take place until the course was clear." The interest shown was hardly surprising as most people had probably never seen an aircraft before.

Towards four o'clock, as the sports drew to a close, a buzz of excitement went through the crowd when Astley and his mechanic appeared. The Birdling was wheeled to one end of the ground, only to be engulfed once more and for some time no progress could be made as the police fought to keep back over-curious spectators. Excitement rose to fever pitch as Astley climbed into his seat and the engine was started. Loud cheers accompanied the take-off run, which at first seemed normal, but soon it became clear the aircraft was failing to leave the ground. As it rapidly approached a high stone wall many people realised they were witnessing a crash rather than a flight.

Adjacent to this wall a cycling track ran the length of the recreation ground, which caused the Birdling to bounce into the air. Its wheels then caught the top of the wall, and as the *North Wales Observer* reported "...there was a huge crash, a volume of smoke and Mr Astley and the monoplane completely disappeared!" He had been thrown out of the cockpit, but luckily escaped without injury, though the aircraft was badly damaged. Spectators rushed to the scene, somebody produced a stretcher and a policeman in his haste to reach the accident jumped from the wall on to rough ground and badly sprained his ankle.

Astley meanwhile got to his feet, calmly lit a cigarette and climbed back over the wall, to receive an ovation from the crowd. Disappointment at the failure to fly was evident but nevertheless he still commanded enormous respect for trying.

Whatever the reason for failure, whether some technical defect or Astley's mishandling, he took a large risk in taking off from an area bounded by a high stone wall. The cycle track's existence proved providential, otherwise a direct collision with the wall might have had more serious consequences. In September 1912 Astley's lack of expertise proved fatal when he was killed giving exhibition flights in Belfast, again from an unsuitable ground.

Two days after the mishap at Pwllheli another aviator, R.A. King, made a flight along the North Wales coast. A more competent pilot than Astley, he took off in his Farman biplane, just after mid-day, from Freshfield's aerodrome between Liverpool and Southport. King's intention was to make a local flight only, but once in the air he decided to emulate Robert Loraine and pay a surprise visit to Colwyn Bay. He followed the coastline, in good weather and one hour later arrived over Colwyn, landing shortly after on the beach.

As usual, the presence of an aircraft, despite its unexpected appearance soon attracted thousands of onlookers. The time of departure was announced to be at 3.30 p.m. but long before then a huge crowd gathered along the promenade and foreshore to watch. At 3.45 p.m. King took off and headed back to Freshfield's having accomplished quite a successful cross-country flight.

Five weeks later he returned to participate in a two week long flying meeting, supposedly to put the locality on the aviation map, but in fact it turned out to be something of a fiasco.

Loraine's and King's flights seemed to have aroused local enthusiasm for aviation and the idea of establishing a permanent flying ground at Rhos-on-Sea, with a grand flying meeting to launch the scheme, gained ready approval. Organising the meeting was E. Mines, of Liverpool, who took a leading part in the organising of the rather unsuccessful 1910 Doncaster meeting, which perhaps did not auger too well for Colwyn Bay.

'The Aeroplane,' for instance, was critical of the dates chosen, July 15th to July 29th, which clashed with the round Britain race arranged for July 22nd to the 27th. This race was organised by the *Daily Mail* and as a prize of £10,000 was at stake, every self respecting aviator would be competing. On the other hand, this could be an advantage by helping to stimulate local interest to an even greater extent, and at least one good pilot, (King), would be on hand.

Another factor to be considered was the forthcoming Royal visit to North Wales, due to commence on July 13th with the investiture of the Prince of Wales at Caernarfon. Two days later the official opening of new university buildings at Bangor by King George V was obviously a special event, and a tour of the region was to follow. Would this detract from, or attract interest in the flying meeting? Further complication arose when rail communications were considerably disrupted by preparations for the Royal visit. Twelve thousand soldiers, for example, had to be transported to Caernarfon, and as they took priority, two aircraft despatched from London to Colwyn Bay did not arrive when expected, having presumably been shunted into a siding somewhere and forgotten.

Whatever the arguments over timings, a site had to be found, and so a large field belonging to Dinerth Hall farm was selected. It adjoined Rhos-on-Sea golf links near the Llandudno — Colwyn Bay road, and henceforth was to be known as Rhos Aerodrome. Two hangars were built, as permanent fixtures because the organisers expected flying would take place every season. A charge of five shillings (25 pence) per week would be made for their use, reduced to one shilling (5 pence) for aviators willing to put up their own hangars.

Other pilots hired, besides King, were A. Cassell Hunt of London, J. G. Booth from Bedford and M. Lefevre. A local man, Vivian Hewitt from Rhyl had been turned down. It was hoped, before the meeting ended, to secure the services of Mr Melly from Liverpool and one of the exhibition circuit stars, Claude Graham White. In the event however only King and Lefevre did any flying.

On July 13th the *Welsh Coast Pioneer* advertised the meeting;

But things went wrong from the start. The missing aircraft, lost en route from London by rail had still not been located and bad weather caused flying to be cancelled from the very first day. Strong winds then blew relentlessly preventing any further flying during the rest of the week. Another problem was ensuring the attendance of large crowds if flying became possible due to improved conditions. Dinerth Hall lay between two main centres of population, Llandudno and Colwyn Bay, and so the arrangement was that a blue flag would be hoisted on the flagpole of the Metropole Hotel, Colwyn Bay and St. George's Hotel, Llandudno if flying was imminent!

Not until Sunday 23rd July did King manage a short flight to Colwyn Bay sands and back. On the following day, despite a strong wind, King was in the air again but prudently he did not venture outside the field's boundary. For the next three days continuing strong winds grounded everyone until Friday evening when conditions became a little calmer. Grasping this opportunity to fly, King was soon airborne. He flew over Rhos golf links, landed near the pier, took off almost immediately, made half a dozen circuits of the bay and came down near his take-off point. Later, he flew to the Great Orme.

The next day, July 29th was the last of the meeting — and produced no flying. The whole fortnight had been a dismal failure from all viewpoints.

However, the idea was not completely abandoned, as three weeks later, King and Lefevre returned to try their luck yet again. Proceedings began on Wednesday, August 16th when Lefevre attempted a flight in his Short Wright biplane but failed to become airborne, because, he said, the propeller had too coarse a pitch. A telegram was sent requesting another which had not arrived by Friday, and so Lefevre, tired of waiting, reshaped the old one himself. This enabled him to make long hops up and down the flying ground.

King had also been active and on Saturday flew in front of a large crowd. His partner, not wanting to miss out, decided that he too would perform, but the aircraft rose only a few feet after its take-off run before the engine seemed to lose power. Lefevre's machine ran into a ditch, throwing him from his seat into the still revolving propeller.

Medical examination revealed broken ribs and internal injuries in addition to severe head bruising. After being in a critical condition for some time Lefevre eventually recovered.

Following this accident, flying at Rhos really did come to an end, and although the flying ground did receive mention in Janes 1912 edition the site remained forgotten until 1927, when its development as a small civil aerodrome came under consideration.

Whilst not strictly within the geographical area of

Gwynedd, it is worth mentioning the flights of Vivian Hewitt at Rhyl, from October 1911 onwards.

Hewitt came from a very wealthy English family (with Welsh connections on his mother's side) and lived at Bodfari, Flintshire. A successful brewing business provided the means by which Hewitt was free of ordinary financial constraints. After developing an interest in aviation he spent some time at Brooklands before returning to North Wales. This appears odd as Brooklands was then an important centre of aviation development; in comparison Wales was an absolute desert.

In February 1911 he purchase a Bleriot and began flying from a field in the Voryd area of Rhyl. A hangar, complete with an extremely well appointed workshop was constructed and from here Hewitt made many flights, becoming a regular sight in the skies of Rhyl. One of his favourite stunts was to fly low over the promenade, dropping cards printed with the words "Dropped by Vivian Hewitt from his Monoplane at Rhyl." This kind of publicity proved beneficial to the resort, making Hewitt a very popular figure with local residents and traders. During the next few years until 1914, he continued to give exhibition flights locally and became the first airman to fly regularly in North Wales. Arguably his greatest achievement was to fly from Holyhead to Dublin in April 1912.

Undoubtedly the best pilot to visit Gwynedd during this early period of aviation was Gustav Hamel. Of German extraction, Hamel's flying exploits had earned him an enviable reputation. He could boast of crossing the English channel eleven times, (twice with a passenger), achieving a world record for height of 11,500 feet, piloting the first aircraft to carry official airmail in Britain, taking part in numerous competitions and races, and giving flying displays unrivalled for their show of skill, plus many other feats which made him one of the most popular aviators in the country. Indeed, the *North Wales Chronicle* gave him the supreme accolade, "premier of the World!"

In February 1913 Hamel received permission from Lord Penrhyn to hold a flying exhibition in the grounds of his home, Penrhyn Castle, Bangor, in return for a percentage of the takings of course. The date was to be Wednesday March 12th.

The organiser of this and other meetings in North Wales was C. E. Hickman of Wrexham, whose souvenir programme informed the people of Bangor that "your town is fortunate in the opportunity of being able to witness such an exhibition as Mr Hamel always gives to his audience. His bankings, vol-planes and pancake descents are extremely thrilling. But these fascinating intricacies along with the beauty and grace of Flying can be seen perfectly only from the Flying Ground, certainly not from the street or roadside" — clearly the risk of reduced takings had to be cut to a minimum!

March the 12th turned out to be exceptionally fine and bright with only a light breeze blowing. Between four and five thousand people were attracted to Penrhyn, and a feature which caused surprise was the large number of cars present — over eighty. What would the organisers think of the vehicles that swamp RAF Valley during present day flying shows?

Prior to Hamel's flight, advertised to take place at 2.30 p.m., his aircraft, a Bleriot monoplane, was on view drawing large crowds as ever. But as time passed and 2.30 approached, the wind, which had been freshening all morning, was blowing strongly enough to make Hamel consider abandoning the flight. He waited until 3.30 p.m., the advertised time of the second flight, and decided, against his better judgement, to fly.

A great cheer went up as the Bleriot was wheeled out of the viewing enclosure to a gentle rise some distance away. The engine was started and the aircraft achieved an easy take-off along the downward sloping ground.

When it reached a height of seventy feet however it was seen to waver momentarily before diving steeply to the ground amidst cries of alarm from spectators. Hamel managed to avoid a full crash, but even so considerable damage was done to the aircraft. Before leaving for London by train later that afternoon he talked of his experience:

"I should never have gone up," he said, "I felt that I was in for a smash. The wind above was very much stronger than on the ground. Just when I got level with the top of the clump of trees...a gust of wind pushed me down to the ground. I dropped a clear seventy feet. I made a great effort to get the machine up and just managed to save myself from being killed by bringing her as gently as I could to earth."

He continued, "I am very disappointed, but it could not be helped. I don't think you could have got another airman to go out on such a day with the wind blowing so hard," — which was probably true enough.

Five months later, undeterred by his accident, Hamel was back in North Wales giving exhibition flights. This time the venue was the Welsh National Agricultural Show held at Portmadoc on August 7th and 8th.

No mishaps marred the proceedings on this occasion and Hamel was undoubtedly the leading attraction of the Show, though he did face a little competition from another attraction, which, according to the *North Wales Observer*, also drew the attention of the crowd — "a stuffed buffalo shown by Mr W. Griffith, representative of the Canadian Government."

The combination of Gustav Hamel and a stuffed buffalo seems to have been irresistible and over 45,000 people passed through the turnstiles. Over the two day period he made several flights in his Bleriot monoplane, and once reached a height of 3,000 feet, which must have been regarded as a remarkable achievement by the onlookers.

Less than a year later, in May 1914, this most courageous of early aviators disappeared in the English Channel on a flight from Paris to London.

The last flying exhibition to be held in the county before the start of World War I, was during the summer of 1914 when Fred Raynham, one of the leading pilots of the day, flew a two seater Bleriot fitted with floats, from Llandudno Bay. Organised by the Daily Mail at a charge of £40 to the Town Council, the event was due to take place on June 5th and 6th but bad weather delayed proceedings as explained by the *Llandudno Advertiser* — "the waterplane flights by Mr Raynham which were to have commenced on Monday, aroused great interest, but unfortunately the weather to a very great extent spoilt what would have been a most successful early season event."

"The waterplane arrived at Llandudno on Thursday by train from Scarborough, and was housed in a hangar that had been erected on a vacant plot of land between the Hippodrome Gardens and Sefton Gate, which had been very kindly lent by Lord Mostyn, who writing to the local committee, expressed his great interest in the exhibition.

The hangar was the centre of interest throughout Friday and Saturday, when the operations of the mechanics were closely watched, and so great was the curiosity that the hangar had to be roped off to keep the spectators from approaching too closely to the waterplane, which was taken to pieces and thoroughly overhauled.

The mechanics were at work throughout Sunday in order that everything may be in readiness for the first flight on Monday morning. The approximate time was eleven o'clock when it was high tide, and the flights could be started within a short distance of the beach from the pier end of the bay. No more picturesque or suitable spot could be imagined than the setting of the beautiful Llandudno Bay, crescent-shaped, with the Great and Little Ormes pushing out into the sea at the extremes and forming natural grand stands."

"Rough weather on Monday and Tuesday; To the great disappointment of the thousands who hoped to see the exhibition by Mr Raynham, the *"Daily Mail"* airman, the weather completely broke down on Monday. At high tide when the first flight was to have been made, huge waves were pounding the shingle and dashing the spray on to the promenade and it would have been disastrous even to have attempted to get the waterplane into the sea. It was hoped that the conditions would moderate with the ebb of the tide, but they grew worse, and heavy rain put the closure on any hopes that may have remained.

Owing to the continued rough weather on Tuesday no flights were possible. The waves were much bigger than on Monday, and the spray was thrown in smoke-like columns to a great height. The spectacle was a magnificent one, but it was most disappointing to the people who came into the town to see the waterplane exhibitions."

The *'Advertiser'* continued with its description of events:—

"Throughout Tuesday night the wind blew with hurricane force, but the morning gave a change, and the announcement was made that there would be flights when the sea subsided. The sea had been very rough, and several motor boats were considerably damaged.

Shortly before four o'clock in the afternoon the waterplane was brought out of the hangar and towed by scores of willing helpers along the half-mile of promenade to the lifeboat slipway, followed by a huge crowd.

The tide was then at half-ebb, and hundreds of men and women, anxious to get into the front row, waded in inches of water heedless of its effect on their footwear.

Mr Raynham having taken his seat, the waterplane cut along the rippling waves for about fifty yards and then rose gracefully in the air.''

After carrying out some simple manoeuvres, much to the satisfaction of the watching crowd, Raynham flew across Llandudno Bay, over the Little Orme and headed towards Colwyn Bay. There he gave flights to a few passengers, met some local dignitaries and "took tea at the Hotel Metropole" before returning to Llandudno.

According to the *'Advertiser'*, "the weather on Thursday morning was magnificent, the sun shining from a cloudless sky, its rays being tempered by a gentle breeze just sufficient to ripple the waters of the bay, which danced and glittered in the genial sunshine."

Raynham proceeded to give a display lasting some twenty minutes before landing in order to take up a passenger, at the not inconsiderable price of £4-4-0 for a flight. The passenger in question was a Miss May Jones of West Shore, Llandudno, whom the *'Advertiser'* described as "a magnificent horsewoman and thorough sportswoman." She was further described as "an ardent supporter of the Suffrage cause, and it is said that she was the first lady to drive a motor car in the city of Birmingham."

"She was loudly applauded on taking her seat, and amid much waving of handkerchiefs the waterplane glided off. The flight terminated with a spiral volplane from a considerable height, and alighted on the water like a seagull. Her friends crowded around her when she stepped ashore, but while waiting for the certificate, Miss Jones told an 'Advertiser' reporter that the spiral volplane was ripping."

"Would you go up again?" interrupted one lady friend.

"I'd only like to get half a chance," was the quick reply, with a slight sigh.

"It's simply great," she continued, "to be up in the air like that. I felt that I never wanted to come down. The whole experience was simply thrilling."

After this Mr Raynham flew round the Great Orme and on to Conway, where the hum of the engine drew every inhabitant of the ancient borough to their doors. On his return he ascended to a very great height, shut off the engine and descended to within a few yards of the water by a daring spiral volplane.

Rising slightly again, he made a switch-back circuit of the bay, within a very few yards of the sea. This last performance delighted the crowd, who went home thoroughly pleased with the morning's flights.

Mr Raynham intended to visit Colwyn Bay in the afternoon, but when the waterplane was being taken out one of the floats was punctured by a stone. Repairs could not be effected in time for Colwyn Bay to be visited, and Mr Raynham returned to London."

It was in fact the last time such flights could be witnessed by the people of Gwynedd before the War put an end to such pleasures for four years.

Chapter 3

AVIATION RESEARCH AT BANGOR

During the early years of this century two academics at Bangor University, Professor G. H. Bryan and W. Ellis Williams, were responsible for producing original work on aerodynamic theory. In addition, Ellis Williams designed, constructed and flew his own aeroplane for experimental purposes at Llanddona, Anglesey.

The story begins in 1896 when the University appointed as professor of mathematics, Dr. George Hartley Bryan, FRS and Fellow of Peterhouse College, Cambridge. He was a man with a keen desire to apply his ideas to practical ends, particularly in the field of aerodynamics. Bryan had been amongst those present at the early experiments of the wealthy American expatriot Sir Hiram Maxim at Baldwyns Park, Kent, with his huge trammelled, steam powered machine.

Stimulated by these experiments and aware of the need for a proper scientific approach to the study of flight, Bryan wrote a lucid and far sighted article in October 1897 for *'Science Progress'* on powered flight. On methods of propulsion, for example, he expressed a view that turbines "may in all likelihood supersede engines with reciprocating parts." Bryan was however referring to steam turbines but nevertheless his vision of the future had a fair measure of accuracy. He also had strong views on the place of theory in the development of flight, observing that "attention has been frequently directed by me to the purely mathematical aspects of the problem of flight with especial reference to their importance in elucidating and supplementing the knowledge obtainable by practical and experimental methods," i.e. a good mix of theory and practice. In 1901 he gave a lecture at the Royal Institution, expressing similar themes.

At this time he was working on a theory of stability and began to collaborate with William Ellis Williams, a recently graduated student from Bangor University, who shared Bryan's interest in aerodynamics.

Ellis Williams, a quarryman's son, was born and bred in Bethesda, just a few miles from Bangor. Rather shy in manner but extremely clever, he had a brilliant career as an undergraduate, winning many prizes and gaining a college fellowship. With his mathematical ability plus a practical approach, he proved an excellent colleague for Bryan. The two worked steadily on their project and in January 1904 the results of their research were published in a Royal Aeronautical Society paper, "The Longitudinal Stabililty of Aeroplane Gliders," which has been subsequently described as the first of the Society's more important papers. Ellis Williams, in addition to being an academic scientist, was, as mentioned before, a practical man, and in order to provide some experimental data and illustration for the 1904 paper he constructed small gliders, to which were attached pieces of magnesium lit just before launching so that the ensuing flight path could be recorded on photographic plates. A slotted rotating wheel was also placed in front of the plates, enabling the velocity of the gliders to be estimated.

Unfortunately, however much merit this theoretical work possessed, it did not gain approval either from other mathematicians or the pioneer aeroplane constructors, who dismissed investigations of this type as irrelevant to their more empirical approach. Naturally enough Bryan and Williams were disappointed by these reactions but persevered with the work, in some isolation, until eventually in 1911 Bryan published his book "Stability in Aviation", which proved to be an influential volume. Writing an introduction to "Aerial Locomotion" by E. H. Harper and A. Ferguson in the same year, and no doubt thinking of his own position, Bryan said, "although there is still a good deal of hostility on the part of some practical men towards workers in pure science there are nevertheless indications that a better state of feeling is beginning to arise and that those who are concerned with the construction and use of aeroplanes are beginning to show greater willingness to pay attention to investigations of a theoretical character which may be likely to suggest directions for further improvement."

As it happened, his ideas were indeed gaining acceptance: at the National Physical Laboratory for example, where a department of aeronautics had been set up, Bryan's theories were used by Leonard Bairstow, (later to become a leading aerodynamicist in the preliminary investigations into stability). The Advisory Committee on Aeronautics said of Bryan's book, "this volume provides the fullest account hitherto given of the theory of the stability of an aeroplane."

Full recognition of Bryan's work came in 1914 when he was awarded the gold medal of the Royal Aeronautical Society — its highest award — given previously only to the Wright brothers in 1909 and Octave Chanute in 1910. Ellis Williams on the other hand did not fare as well, being surprisingly rejected, along with many others equally well qualified, for membership of the Society in 1911, but amends were made in 1912, when he was elected an Associate Fellow.

His academic career, after graduation, had taken him to the universities of Glasgow and then Munich, where he worked under the famous Professor Rontgen. In 1906 he was appointed assistant lecturer in physics at Bangor where he remained for the rest of his life, becoming, in 1943, the first Professor of Electrical Engineering in the University of Wales.

After his appointment Williams continued to collaborate with Professor Bryan on mathematical theories of flight, in between pursuing other academic interests. Then, in 1909, when the practical problems of flight had been solved he decided to build his own machine in order to conduct aerodynamic experiments. The *Daily Post* described his purpose as, "the furtherance of his study of the stability and efficiency of flying machines and to obtain experimental data for a theory of their motion."

The challenge and interest of construction for its own sake was probably just as appealing as the prospect of some actual flying, albeit of a gentle nature. As the *Daily Post* went on to say, "Mr Williams does not intend to attempt any long or high flight, his object being mainly experimental." Design work commenced in 1909, with assistance provided by Professor Bryan. During the autumn construction of the aircraft began on the premises of Bangor University.

This aircraft however cannot be claimed as the first to be designed and built in Wales as that honour must go to C. H. Watkins who began building his monoplane, delightfully named "Robin Goch" (Red Robin), at Maerdy, Cardiff in 1907. On the other hand Ellis Williams's machine was one of the first in the country conceived purely as a vehicle for research purposes only.

The design was of a monoplane of wooden construction with a span of 32 feet and a length of 37 feet, the framework being triangular or A-shaped in cross section, resting on two long skids, each carrying a wheel. The wings were of 200 square feet in area and were thicker than usual, obtaining a maximum thickness of 8 inches. Ailerons were provided. The aerofoil section was similar to Wing No. 7 used by Eiffel in his experiments on the distribution of pressure (see "La Resistance De L'air et L'Aviation, G. Eiffel, Paris 1910, translated by J. C, Hunsaker 1913), i.e. a curved upper surface and flat lower surface with sharp leading and trailing edges. A lifting tail was used, consisting of a large triangular shaped structure of about 45 square feet in area, with a rectangular rudder above. Power was to be provided by a 35 h.p. air cooled engine. Materials used in construction were ash and bamboo, and the total weight was expected to be 700 pounds. At this time also (December 1909) Ellis Williams published an article in '*Aeronautics*' on the question of the centre of gravity in an aircraft, which more than likely was the result of his own recent design experience, and a useful way of contributing to the scientific debate on the subject.

One very important consideration was that of obtaining adequate finance. With limited means at his disposal Ellis Williams plainly had to keep costs down to a minimum. The obvious course of action was to find someone with money to put into the project. Luckily, a local benefactor was found without too much difficulty — Henry Rees Davies, of Treborth, one of the wealthiest men in the area. His family were the founders and owners of the Menai Bridge shipping line and timber importing business from which they had accumulated enormous wealth. As it happened, Henry Davies was keenly interested in aviation and was more than willing to give financial assistance to the project. He was also a most generous benefactor of Bangor University generally and later in his life took a leading part in its affairs, besides being the author of the well-known and authoritative book: *The Conway and the Menai Ferries*.

On October 29th 1909 his first contribution was £50 towards the cost of a second-hand engine, and, as he said, "to make good our partnership." Ellis William's reply three days later reveals the state of progress on the aircraft, as work had commenced before these financial matters were settled — "I beg to acknowledge receipt of £50 and to tell you how grateful I am to you for offering to join in the enterprise... With regard to the engine I bought it from Mr Pillion, a capitalist...!" Unfortunately there is no record of the engine type.

"I have obtained a piece of ash for the propeller and am now shaping it for the blades. I can then fit it on the engine and get a proper test on the horse power which is guaranteed as 40. I have obtained a bit of bamboo suitable for building the frame from Jacob Young... The aluminium castings for holding them together I can make here. The chassis and engine frame will best be of ash... I dare say you have noticed that in this week's *Flight* that the latest Antoinette is made with a section of supporting surface very similar to the one I thought of using so that I think we are on safe ground in adopting one with a flat lower and curved upper surface.

Yours etc.

W. E. Williams."

As a result of his interest in aviation Davies wanted an aircraft built to his own design and his letters at this time were full of questions and requests for advice on technical points, for example, he writes in April 1910... "I should like to have a try on a safe machine, but it must be a safe machine with a tendency to keep the right side up and no 'tother way like the Bleriot. Engine and pilot well down below... thought of asking Short Brothers whether they could design a practical ship on these lines... How is the Bamboo Bird? Have you tried her legs yet?"

In fact the framework was completed and on April 5th the engine and propeller were tested, evidently to Ellis Williams' satisfaction as he wrote, "it went very well with little vibration."

Davies meanwhile had visited the Aero Exhibition at Olympia and was most concerned about prices — "a Bleriot for £475 and Handley Page wanted £374 for a concern I wouldn't be seen flying over a ploughed field in. I didn't see a practical biplane under £600 and the best ran up to £1,000." He went on to say that he was keen to do a little flying himself, but suspicious of amateur construction: "not on a homemade bird," and asked Ellis Williams if he would care to design an aircraft, to be built by Short Brothers, for which he would be willing to pay up to £700, "as my contribution to the upward movement." There is no record of any such machine being designed and it is probably fair to say that his ideas represented more of a passing phase aroused by the freshness and excitement of flying rather than a genuine passion or commitment to aviation. However, he gave every assistance to Ellis Williams in his efforts to bring his project to fruition.

The next step after construction of the aircraft was completed was to locate a suitable operating site. The generally hilly nature of the region confined any search to the coastal strip and the flatter areas of Anglesey, where Davies thought it unlikely that a suitable field could be found; but in his view the broad expanse of firm sand at Red Wharf Bay on the south east side of the island would make a good site. Interestingly enough, the only mainland coastal site suggested by Davies, between Abergele and Rhyl, was also chosen some 40 years later in 1953 by the Ministry of Civil Aviation and Welsh Advisory Council as suitable for the development (which never took place) of a small grass airfield to serve North Wales.

Ellis Williams agreed with his friend on the attractions of the Red Wharf Bay site. The hard and level sand, about 2½ miles long and one mile broad, was ideal for his purpose, and so he set about choosing a spot to build a small hangar, selecting a patch of ground close to the village of Llanddona. The landowner, Sir Harry Verney, gave his permission for building to take place, adding, "I am delighted to hear of the enterprise which Mr Williams is showing," and so the hangar was put up, adjoining a cottage known as Bwlch y Ffoes Bach, only a few yards from the beach.

By June 1910 the aircraft was nearly complete with only work on the controls and wheels still outstanding. Ellis Williams had in fact considered fitting floats, but faced with design problems and excessive weight he accepted Davies's advice: "the float arrangements are more difficult to work out than might appear at first...I am afraid your only chance of getting into the air this season is off the ground."

The local press set an optimistic tone in their reports: "The new all Welsh aeroplane is being constructed on exact and profound mathematical principles and it will be interesting to note how the young aviator who at present has absolutely no practical knowledge or experience of flying will, when he has learnt (as he intends to do) succeed in his attempts...Professor Bryan remarked there was no reason why, given a sufficiently powerful engine (which, however, Mr Williams cannot at present afford) the machine should not make a flight from Holyhead to Dublin. It may be added that Mr Williams has the fullest confidence in the success of his machine and proposes to make his first attempts in July."

As stated previously, economy had been a prime consideration in the building of the aircraft and it is interesting to see that costs from October 1909 to March 1910 amounted to £138-6-9d. with the engine, as the account shows, at £100, being by far the most expensive item. The final cost is not known but is unlikely to have been much more. The hangar also was built as cheaply as possible, using second-hand materials, with a total cost under £30, leading Henry Davies to remark, "I see you are **plotting out the shed with the same economy with which you have put together the machine. I wonder what it would** cost me to put up a shed?" During the summers that followed, this hangar became Ellis Williams's home as **well as that of his** mechanic (whose identity is unfortunately not known), and his address for correspondence:— "The Aeroplane Shed, Llanddona, Anglesey.!"

As completion of the aircraft approached, the problem of transporting it from Bangor to Llanddona arose. No precise information is available on how the removal was accomplished, or even the date. However, a letter written by Davies on June 27th 1910 provides a strong clue when he offered the use of his launch to move materials for the hangar to Llanddona.

"If you could charter some old boat to take them, our launch could tow her round on a fine day or possibly one of the large fishing boats would take everything" (meaning the aircraft?) "round under her own sail." He wrote again a month later on July 27th, "the launch will be available next week if required..." The edition of the *North Wales Observer* for August 12th provides a little more information… "Only a part of the monoplane which has been built by Mr W. E. Williams… has been removed to Red Wharf Bay, Anglesey, where experiments in aviation are to be conducted shortly."

Probably the wings and framework were separated for transportation and re-assembled at Llanddona during August, with an attempt at flying taking place in September — judging from the *North Wales Observer* for August 26th which only mentions that experiments are to take place and that the hangar was being erected.

The arrival of an aircraft in Llanddona was regarded with awe and apprehension by the local inhabitants, particularly some of the older ones, who had lived their lives in the calm of the previous century. On the other hand it had a magnetic attraction for the village's youths, who would gather to watch whenever a test run was imminent. Often they would assist in the process of manoeuvring the machine in and out of the hangar, or recovering it when failure had occurred some distance along the beach, to be rewarded for their efforts by a penny or two.

In fact this happened all too frequently, and Ellis Williams's high hopes of carrying out his experiments that summer were soon dashed altogether by the aircraft's failure to fly. This was due to a combination of an insufficiently powerful engine and a too heavy airframe, but Williams remained undeterred and spent the next four summers, until the outbreak of World War I, struggling to obtain some experimental results from his aircraft. However, he neglected to keep a record of tests made, weather conditions, dates etc. and so a detailed day-to-day account is more or less non-existent.

For example, there is only one specific date mentioned when a successful flight took place and many other gaps remain such as details of test runs, but luckily two photographs, both undated, have been unearthed. They show clearly that extensive modification took place, posing the obvious question — which is the earlier model?

Unmodified aircraft

Modified aircraft

*Monoplanes designed and built by W. E. Williams at Llanddona,
Anglesey, 1910-1914*

Photograph 1 shows an ungainly, heavy looking aircraft with the triangular tail and wing tips missing. Photograph 2 shows a machine with the wings and tail but the large A-shaped framework replaced by what appears to be a single bamboo spar, the length of the chassis considerably cut down, and the two skids replaced by a single central skid, resulting in a much simplified, lighter looking structure.

Which then is the earlier of the two machines? Bearing in mind the description given in the *Daily Post* of June 23rd 1910, of the A-shaped framework and two long skids, and the *North Wales Observers'* view on August 12th that, "the machine...appears to be considerably heavier than the ordinary type of flying machine," plus the fact that the aircraft failed to fly that season, it is probable that photograph 1 shows the early model, which after the failure of 1910 was radically modified and lightened, and the model seen in photograph 2 is the result.

Of course it is not possible to assess, in the absence of further evidence, whether this was the final version or whether there was subsequent modification.

During the summers of 1911 and 1912 Ellis Williams was in correspondence with A. V. Roe, Handley Page and Weston Hurlin regarding the purchase of secondhand items such as wheels, propellers, undercarriage parts, wire etc. and so this was the likeliest time that major changes took place in the design of the aircraft. Additional evidence is given by contemporary eye witness accounts which tell of trial runs followed by lengthy periods spent in the hangar when it was clear that much work was being done on the machine. Proof of failure, and its possible cause comes from one of Ellis Williams's correspondents, a Mr Hope of Swinton, Manchester, with whom he had been in touch regarding another engine. Hope wrote on October 1st, "I am very sorry that you were unable to fly with your machine, but I was afraid that you would find that the engine could not develop sufficient power." In fact, engine design lagged behind airframe design, with the result that early aircraft were powered (or under-powered) by weak, unreliable engines, and in Ellis Williams's particular case the combination of such an engine, and second-hand at that, plus a heavy airframe was too much. Obtaining a suitable engine occupied much of his time and a great deal of correspondence took place between himself and those with engines to sell such as A. V. Roe and Weston Hurlin.

Mr Hope was in touch again during November, stating that the engine he had in mind for the monoplane was a Gnome type and in the course of his letter said, "as to the Aviation School, I am afraid we could not arrange anything before next spring." It seems that Ellis Williams, aware of his total lack of experience in handling an aircraft, hoped to have some flying instruction and thereby increase his chances of success at Llanddona. Again, as with many other details, there is no record that he actually did so.

The month of June 1911 saw him preparing his second article for *Aeronautics*, this time dealing with the stresses imposed on aircraft framework, and quite obviously based on the experiences with his own machine. The preliminaries for the coming flying season began when he was in contact with A. V. Roe at Manchester regarding the hire of an engine.

He decided upon either a 35 h.p. JAP or 40 h.p. ENV, eventually choosing the JAP. A. V. Roe agreed on July 11th to hire out the engine for two months, supplying also the propeller plus petrol and oil tanks. It was duly delivered, and after purchasing some additional wood and fabric Ellis Williams was ready for his next attempt at flying.

Sometime in August or early September (the actual date is not known) success came when the monoplane made its maiden flight. Unfortunately no record exists of such details as duration, speed and height achieved, neither is it known if any experimental work was carried out. A. V. Roe, eager to maintain contact, wrote in mid-September, "we hope you are getting on satisfactorily with your experiments. When we were using the 35 h.p. JAP we used to get between 200 and 220 lbs thrust but since then the engine has been thoroughly overhauled and extra long pistons have been added to stop the oil being thrown out.

Please be sure to give the engine plenty of oil, otherwise it soon slows up. You should get about 1500 revs." However this advice came too late as by then the crankshaft had broken, and the engine had to be returned for repair, thus bringing an end to the experimental programme for that year. At the same time, Ellis Williams booked an engine for Easter 1912, hoping that his luck would improve then.

November 1911 saw the publication of another article for *Aeronautics* — "A New Method for the Measurement of Air Resistance on Planes and Curved Surfaces." Inspired by Eiffel's recent book, it criticised the research methods of other workers, and offered an alternative method.

During the winter months Ellis Williams also turned his mind to practical things such as the idea of using copper gills to improve engine cooling. The critical problem was attachment of the gills to the cylinder walls as the slightest gap meant a serious decrease in the cooling properties of the gills, thereby defeating the object of their existence in the first place. A. V. Roe were asked for their opinion and possible help in persuading an engine manufacturer to adopt the idea, but their reply was discouraging. The idea was not new and had been tried before in 1902, on the Aster engine fitted to the Aerial Motor Tricycles for example, and as it did not catch on then, it was thought highly unlikely that a manufacturer would consider any proposition for further development.

On March 26th, 1912 A. V. Roe notified Ellis Williams that they had sold the engine used by him during the previous summer, but they were informing him in good time so that arrangements could be made for the hire of another engine. However, he already was in communication with a number of other people in his search for a suitable engine at a suitable price. Mr Brooks of Huddersfield had a Bleriot type monoplane for example, powered by a 35 h.p. JAP for sale at £65; Planes Ltd. of Birkenhead had a 60 h.p. Green at £150; and Weston Hurlin Ltd. of Paddington a similar engine at £100.

A letter by Ellis Williams to Planes Ltd. in March reveals his problem, "in reply to yours of the 23rd inst. re Green engine, I intend to use it in an aeroplane which I have here. The machine was successfully flown last summer with a JAP engine which, though going well, (omitting the fact that the crankshaft had broken) was not quite powerful enough for long flights and hence I thought of trying with a higher Horse Power this year." By now it was too late to attempt any flying during Easter and the next attempt would have to wait until summer when Ellis Williams would be free of his University duties. He redoubled his efforts to locate an engine and even asked the editor of *Aeronautics* if he could assist. The editor agreed and came up with an almost new 30 h.p. Clement-Bayard at £75 and a 35 h.p. Green at £100 neither of which was suitable, as the first was too small and the second too expensive. Eventually, after considerable letter writing and negotiation extending from the end of March until May with Weston Hurlin Ltd. a 45 h.p. REP was selected and a hire charge of £20 for three months agreed, with the option of purchase by payment of another £25.

Subsequently Ellis Williams changed his mind and decided to have a 40 h.p. Clement instead. The company took their time delivering the engine, much to his annoyance as he was anxious to restart work on the project. Requests for an explanation resulted in various excuses and it was not until July 20th that the engine was finally despatched. There is no record of any successful flight taking place during the following weeks unfortunately. A surprise came on September 5th when a letter was received from the solicitors of a Mr J. Briere, Baker Street, London who had forwarded his Clement engine to Weston Hurlin in May on a sale or return basis. Repeated applications for the return of his property elicited no response, which was quite understandable, as the engine had been hired out for three months to Ellis Williams! The situation was evidently not good at the company as he received a letter on September 6th from an employee mentioning business difficulties and enquiring if he was in need of an assistant. By early October the solicitors had obtained judgement against the company and the matter was resolved when Ellis Williams offered Briere £25 for the engine. The offer was accepted — Briere received his money, Ellis Williams kept the engine, and Weston Hurlin eventually went out of business.

The next flying season, that of summer 1913, was more successful and provides the only specific date when it is known flying for experimental purposes took place, and gives an insight into the research methods utilised. The flight took place on September 3rd at sunset in conditions approaching a flat calm when a speed of 37 miles per hour was reached at an estimated height of 7 feet. Duration and distance were not recorded. The purpose of the flight and the whole experimental programme at this time was to investigate pressure distribution on a wing and then to compare results with wind tunnel tests on a model of a similar wing. In fact these experiments were a duplication of Eiffel's tests made in his Paris laboratory. Small holes had been drilled in a series of model wings of varying aerofoil section, and rubber tubing inserted, which was then connected to a manometer in order to determine the pressure at various points from leading edge to trailing edge. The problem was determining the validity of data thus obtained when applied to the design of full scale wings, i.e. discovering if allowance had to be made for a conversion factor when scaling up from models.

Ellis Williams hoped that his experiments would reveal a high degree of correlation between results obtained from full size wing tests and those of models in a wind tunnel, thus proving the value of models in research work and design. Such a correlation had already been observed in Eiffel's experiments, as pointed out by J. C. Hunraker in his 1913 translation of La Resistance De L'Air et L'Aviation — "the concordance between model tests and the latest tests on full sized aeroplanes are considered remarkable, and appear to be a final verification and justification of M. Eiffel's laboratory methods." In similar fashion to the Frenchman's method Ellis Williams attached an aluminium strip with twelve brass tubes in it between two ribs on the wing of his aircraft. These tubes penetrated through holes in the fabric and rubber tubing then connected them to a manometer incorporating a camera-like device using photographic paper to record the results. This equipment was housed in the cockpit and in addition included an inclinometer to measure the wing's angle of incidence.

The aircraft was flown straight and level only a few feet above the ground in order to minimise the effects of any eddies, but Ellis Williams conceded that the 'cushioning' aspect of being so close to the ground might possibly influence the airflow and pressure distribution.

The comparison tests on a model were carried out in a wind tunnel of his own construction (it had a 4 foot diameter and air was drawn through by a 7 h.p. motor). When the model wing was placed near the tunnel floor to recreate the effect of flying just a few feet above the ground it was found that the direct effect of the floor masked the effect of the wing and spoilt the comparison to a certain extent. But nevertheless enough information was available to reach the conclusion, "that wind channel experiments may be relied on to give accurate results when applied to actual full scale machines." Details of the flight and experimental procedure were published in the *Aeronautical Journal* for October 1914, and it also remains the only detailed account of these experiments.

Ellis Williams was not the only investigator of these problems. Similar work on pressure distribution had been carried out at the National Physical Laboratory by B. Melville Jones and C. J. Paterson, who used brass models of an aerofoil. Their experimental methods were much more rigorously scientific however. The results were published in March 1913 in the Technical Report of the Adivsory Committee for Aeronautics for 1912-13 under the title, "Investigation of the Distribution of Pressure over the entire surface of an aerofoil."

There is no record of any further experimental work taking place at Llanddona during the summer of 1914. When the war came Ellis Williams gave up his research activities and spent the war period as an examiner at the Vickers aeroplane factory at Brooklands. Eventually he returned to his academic career at Bangor but by 1919 he felt that he had made his contribution to aviation, which of course had made great strides during the war. His interest in the subject diminished and he turned to fresh endeavours and new challenges such as hydro-electricity and radio.

Meanwhile, his colleague of many years, Professor Bryan, left Bangor in 1917 to continue his work on aerodynamic theory at a number of research establishments. At the end of a three year period he published what were to be the last of his papers on aerodynamics — "The Rigid Dynamics of Circling Flight" (1921) and "The Theory of Initial Motions and its Applications to the Aeroplane" (1922) for instance.

In 1926 he retired and went to live in Italy but died there two years later, aged 64. Ellis Williams on the other hand remained in his native Dyffryn Ogwen until his death in 1962 at the age of 81.

The question arises, did these two men make any significant contribution to the development of aviation? The answer must be yes. In the field of aerodynamic science their early work on the mathematical theory of flight was undoubtedly original and established a base upon which others could build: Herman Glauert of RAE Farnborough for one, whose summary in 1921 of all knowledge on stability and control stemmed from the Bryan and Williams paper of 1903. The aerodynamicist Professor L. Bairstow acknowledged the worth of their association when he wrote in 1939, "the study of the stability and motions of aircraft was given a great initial impetus by the work of Bryan and Williams, starting in 1903 these two workers laid down the fundamental mathematical equations..."

The experiments at Llanddona are not quite in the same category however. Without doubt Ellis Williams can be credited with the design and construction of one of the first aircraft in Wales, which in addition was rather unique in that its purpose was to be a research vehicle but sadly, in the light of these considerations, it was unfortunate that the aircraft's performance turned out to be so inadequate. Hampered by lack of a suitably powerful engine and the need for major changes in design Ellis Williams seems to have expended more effort on modification than experimentation. Getting the aircraft to fly became his main preoccupation, leaving little room for research. The machine itself has no scientific or technical significance, but has historical interest as one of the first, if not the first, aircraft in Britain built purely for aerodynamic research. But to return to Llanddona, Ellis Williams's departure did not mean the end of aircraft construction. In August 1914 the hangar was taken over by another would-be constructor, one Albert Roberts of Llanrwst. Mystery surrounds this man and all that is known about him comes from just a few letters and the memory of an elderly relative.

He certainly chose a bad time to start on his work at Llanddona as the war brought to an end the hitherto unbridled freedom of aircraft constructors to do as they pleased. Restrictions were imposed by the government and Roberts, like others, had to inform the military authorities of his plans. This did not please him greatly judging by his letter to the Army's Western Command HQ at Chester, written on August 22nd...

"While I was at Bangor making certain enquiries I was informed that the Government or Military authorities ought to be acquainted with the nature of the work I am about to commence. I fail to follow or see the necessity of such a course however I decided to follow the advice after receiving the (your) address from the Valuation Office, Caernarvon.

I have taken over an Aeroplane Shed at the above address (Llanddona) where I intend to build a Biplane, the returns from which, I hope, will help me to continue in the pursuance of new Aeronautical ideas.

I expect it will be slow work as I shall work single-handed.

A. Ll. Roberts."

He might well have taken over Ellis Williams's aircraft also, although there is no record of its eventual fate.

Western Command HQ decided that the local police should check the bona fides of Roberts before allowing any aircraft construction to take place. The police did so, and evidently were satisfied that all was in order, but the populance generally was far from satisfied as strong rumours circulated that Roberts was a spy for the Germans, passing messages to submarines in the Irish Sea! He had secretive and solitary ways which did not help to dispel such fears and apparently a close watch was kept on his activities.

No evidence exists that the biplane he spoke of was ever built and the 'new aeronautical ideas', whatever they were, probably remained untested. Sometime during the war Roberts left Llanddona and a sale was arranged at which the principal commodity offered was a large quantity of wood. The hangar was dismantled and sold to a nearby farm where some sections are still in use today.

Aeroplane Account

1909		£	s	d
Oct.	Aeroplane Engine, P. Pillion	100	0	0
Nov 10	Central Novelty Co. — Magnalium & C.	1	5	0
Dec 3	Central Novelty Co. — Propeller Plates	3	0	0
Dec 16	Rubery Owen & Co- Propeller Plates	1	0	4
Dec 30	Rubery Owen & Co-Bolts & Plates		11	8
Dec 20	W.. Evans — Engine Coil	5	4	0
1910				
Jan 7	Young & Co — Bamboos	8	17	4
Jan 31	Rubery Owen & Co — Steel	2	0	0
Feb 25	Rubery Owen & Co — Wire & C.	2	0	0
March 10	Rubery Owen & Co — Wire & C.	2	0	0
March	Watkin Jones & Son — Timber	3	11	8
	Handley Page		8	9
	Penlon Yard — Iron		3	6
	Labour			
	Joiner:- Jan 11th 7/6, Jan 18th 20/-, Feb 4th 25/-,	2	12	6
	Smith:- Feb 18th 21/-, 28th 27/-, March 5th 27/-, March 12th 27/-	5	2	0
March 12	H. Traun & Sons — Ebonite		8	0
	Josiah Hughes		2	0
		137	18	0
			8	9

Aircraft construction costs 1909-1910: a copy of the account kept by W. E. Williams during the building of his monoplane.

An early aeroplane display at Pwllheli: before and after.

Astley at Pwllheli, 1911 — "on the way to disaster.

Astley after the crash.

R.A. King at Colwyn Bay 1911.

Gustav Hamel

Gustav Hamel at Porthmadog in 1913 in his Bleriot Monoplane.

A copy of Gustav Hamel's Souvenir Programme.

A photograph in the 'Llandudno Advertiser' proclaiming the arrival of Mr Reynham who would be flying in his waterplane above the town, and taking passengers at a fee of £4.45 per flight.

The waterplane in flight.

R. A. King: who flew from Southport to Colwyn Bay in 1911.

W. E. Williams in front of the Aeroplane Shed at Llanddona 1910/14.

W. E. Williams

A cartoon of W. E. Williams with his aircraft (from U.C.N.W. Magazine: 'The Mascot', December 1913)

Prof. G.H. Bryan

Robert Loraine about to take off on the first attempted crossing of the Irish Sea, September 11th, 1910.

Robert Loraine taking off from Rhos-on-Sea, August 1910.

Loraine's plane at Rhos-on-Sea, 1910.

Loraine's Biplane at Llanfair-yng-Nghornwy.

Captain Vivian Hewitt on Rhyl Sands, 1912.

Arthur Brown (Mechanic to Capt. V. Hewitt) in 1912 with aeroplane built at The Warren House, Bodffari.

Presentation to Capt. V. Hewitt from the town of Rhyl at the Pavilion Gardens to celebrate his successful crossing of the Irish Sea, 1912.

Chapter 4

CROSSING THE IRISH SEA

Embarking on a flight over the sea during aviation's early years was fraught with danger. Engines were notoriously unreliable, aids to navigation and communication, now taken for granted, were then non-existent, no co-ordinated rescue services were available and weather forecasting was often indifferent. Any aviator contemplating a flight of this kind therefore had to be prepared to accept considerable risks, much more so than on a cross-country flight. Louis Bleriot paved the way, with his historic crossing of the English Channel on July 25th, 1909, taking 37 minutes to fly the 23 miles from Calais to Dover, thus winning immortality for himself and £1,000 from the *'Daily Mail'*.

The Irish Sea crossing, although perhaps less world shattering, presented a more formidable problem. To reach Ireland by aeroplane the pioneer aviator had a choice of four routes — the shortest, from Fishguard to Wexford, secondly, from the Llŷn Peninsula to Wicklow, thirdly, the traditional 60 mile sea route from Holyhead to Dublin. The fourth possibility was a two stage flight from Lancashire to the Isle of Man, and then to Co. Down.

The idea of a cash prize for the first aerial crossing came as early as January 1909, in this letter to *Flight* magazine:—

"Sir,

Mr W. Wright has succeeded in flying a distance of about 80 miles. This is more than sufficient to cover the stretch of water between Holyhead and Dublin and the idea has occurred to us that a successful flight between the two places would excite an immense amount of interest.

We should be glad to contribute £100 to a prize fund to the first to accomplish this feat during 1909 ...

Yours etc.

Mecredy, Percy & Co."

Motor News Office
Dublin.

The prize would have to be substantially improved to attract anyone as Lord Northcliffe's *Daily Mail* was offering £1,000 for a crossing of the 20 mile wide English Channel! No challenger came forward in 1909 but during August 1910 an attempt was made by Robert Loraine, a colourful, flamboyant aviator of the period, to fly from Holyhead to Dublin.

The story of this attempt is an intriguing one of dogged persistence in the face of adversity, incompetence, argument, frustration, wastefulness, and humour.

Loraine was a famous actor cum aviator, whose complex character embraced a taste for action and adventure. Having seen Henry Farman fly in January 1908 and Louis Bleriot in 1909, his imagination was fired and he decided to learn to fly at the earliest opportunity his acting commitments allowed — April 1910. He went to Bleriot's school at Pau and Farman's school in Mourmelons, France, where he gained his pilot's certificate in June 1910. Whilst there Loraine purchased one of Farman's racing biplanes and also persuaded the school's chief mechanic, Jules Vedrines, to accompany him to Britain at a monthly salary of £150.

Vedrines, a fierce, aggressive, working class Parisian, was essentially a frustrated pilot, thwarted in his ambition to fly by lack of money. Loraine's offer enabled him to save enough money to buy an aircraft. Meanwhile he developed his talents as a mechanic and later, in Anglesey, his skills proved of inestimable value.

After attending the Bournemouth flying meeting in July 1910 Loraine moved on to the next, to be held at Blackpool during the first week of August. At this time he

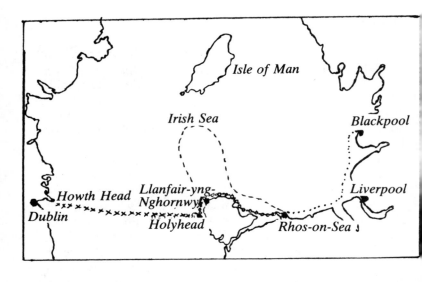

Flights carried out by Robert Loraine, August & September 1910

· · · · · · · Flight from Blackpool to Rhos-on-Sea, August
10th 1910

ᴓᴑᴑᴑᴑᴓᴑ Intended path of flight from Rhos-on-Sea to
Holyhead August 10th 1910

- - - - - - Flight path eventually flown, (approx. only — the
actual path was never accurately plotted)

ᵡᵛᵡᵛᵡᵡᵡ Flight from Holyhead to Howth Head, September
11th 1910

decided to adopt the pseudonym Jones, apparently to prevent his flights being mistaken for theatrical publicity stunts. However, few actors willingly shun the limelight, and when the papers discovered his true identity, the result was increased publicity.

Loraine's team consisted of Vedrines, his brother Emil, supposedly as a carpenter and rigger, but in reality, only a sweetener for Vedrines after he complained of being lonely, and George Smart, the playwright and a close friend, who agreed to manage Loraine's aviation affairs.

At Blackpool he made some good flights, e.g. winning the 'time in air' competition (2 hours and 15 minutes). This success boosted Loraine's confidence sufficiently for him to consider many other, more daring exploits, including a flight over the mountains of Snowdonia — an extremely hazardous if not downright foolhardy plan. Vedrines, never slow to criticize, remarked, "what a damned idea, the poor biplane!"

A crossing of the Irish Sea was then suggested, by the Isle of Man route, which prospect made Loraine wildly enthusiastic. But Vedrines did not think the Farman could withstand two oversea flights in quick succession and the idea was dropped. Smart thought the Holyhead — Dublin route better and bought the others round to his way of thinking with minimum persuasion.

No public announcement was made as Loraine, with his actor's temperament and strong sense of the dramatic, wished to maximise the sensational effect of his flight.

The intention was to reach Holyhead from Blackpool by following the North Wales coast, thus ensuring almost foolproof navigation. Then, on Salt Island, near the harbour, a hangar was to be built for the biplane, and it would be from here that the flight to Dublin would begin. A fleet of six boats were to be hired, and instructed to space themselves out at seven mile intervals along the route as a navigational aid and an on the spot rescue service!

An opportunity to start came with good weather during the second week of August. On Wednesday the 10th Loraine took off from Blackpool at 6.30 a.m. and headed for the North Wales coast. However, as he continued his journey large banks of mist obscured the coastline but nevertheless a sufficiently accurate course was followed. Another worrying problem was the Farman's continuous tendency to climb, which could only be checked by pushing hard on the elevator. "When I did this," he said, "the lever bent like a bow drawn to the full and the strain set up throughout the whole structure was alarming." The fault lay with Emil Vedrines, who adjusted the control wires incorrectly.

Loraine at one point thought of giving up but the sight of the Welsh mountains spurred him on. Then, when he saw the obvious landmark of the Great Orme, having been airborne for an hour and a half and not wishing to push his luck further Loraine decided to land on a golf course. It was in fact Rhos-on-Sea golf course, and by virtue of this flight Loraine became the first airman to fly in North Wales.

As the biplane came to a halt, a man, clad in pyjamas and waving a toothbrush ran out of the clubhouse! He turned out to be the club secretary. To see an aircraft land on the fairway must have given him the surprise of his life. He treated his unexpected guest to breakfast whilst the biplane was cordoned off to await the attentions of Vedrines — following by car from Blackpool.

News of the flight spread like wildfire through Rhos and within an hour several hundred arrived to watch and wonder. The manager of the local tramway lost no time in putting on a special service from Colwyn Bay and Llandudno. During the course of the day thousands visited the golf course.

Whilst waiting for Vedrines to arrive Loraine passed the time pleasantly enough giving interviews to the press, signing autographs and generally being stared at by admiring crowds.

In the early afternoon Vedrines finally arrived and got to work immediately preparing the Farman for the next stage. Loraine announced that he would leave for Holyhead at 5.00 p.m. but long before that hour an immense crowd had gathered.

After a successful take-off he headed towards the Great Orme and Anglesey, again navigating by following the coastline. Within half an hour he should have reached Holyhead, where Smart waited anxiously, having laid out lines of white cloth to mark the landing point. However there was no sign at all of Loraine who had in the meantime become lost somewhere over the Irish Sea. After leaving Rhos he intended to save time by flying directly from the Great Orme to Point Lynas but haze obscured the Anglesey coastline making navigation difficult. His biographer explains further — "crowd worship had dulled his sense of precaution. He had also been incredibly fatigued by the two and a half hours waiting (for the crowds at Rhos to clear a path — a point open to doubt, and completely absent from contemporary press reports). Once in the air he had flown on and on out to sea, dreaming." Loraine's own excuse was that he fell asleep!

"I awoke to find that there was no sign of land," he wrote. "Not a ship in sight to break the solitude only unreal water which glistened here and there where the heat haze did not obscure it. The compass tied to my left hand strut was useless owing to the vibration of my engine and the deviation caused by my magneto. Where was I? I had no instruments to tell me what my course should be. My wrist watch told that my petrol tank was more than half empty. I felt rather a fool and that I was justifying the many accusations against me of recklessness. Where could I be?"

Later he calculated that he was heading for the Isle of Man. By gaining height and using the sun's position as a rough guide, he took a course which he hoped might take him to Anglesey. Luckily the biplane's Gnome engine was running well, though its fuel supply was almost exhausted.

"I felt a little lonely but the sunset colours imparted a sense of cosmic serenity. If death came now at least it would be at the end of a perfect day. Then suddenly Anglesey jumped into view just where I expected it to be."

A mile from shore, with every drop of petrol used, the engine stopped. Loraine glided down to make a heavy landing on rough ground near Bryn Goelcerth farm, Llanfair-yng-Nghornwy, a remote spot on the island's north west coast.

He remained confident that the flight could be continued on the following day without any difficulty, and Smart was instructed to send out the six marker boats as planned. However the wind blew strongly all day making it impossible to fly.

As usual, curious onlookers soon descended upon Bryn Goelcerth in their hundreds. The farmer, with commendable business sense, lost no time in arranging to sell refreshments — 3d (1p.) for a glass of water (from a hidden spring near the farmhouse) and 1/- (5p.) for a glass of milk. Then Smart arrived from Holyhead to see the area for himself. He did not like what he saw, describing Llanfair-yng-Nghornwy as "a strip of wilderness that could only be reached by eight miles of execrable cart tracks." He foresaw many problems, but Loraine on the other hand, remained optimistic. Had he known how frustrating the coming weeks were going to be he might well have felt otherwise.

A pig caused the first problem by eating a bucketful of dope, with which Vedrines was about to coat the Farman's wings. The pig, having eaten its fill then leant against the aircraft's tail and damaged it. Then the six marker boats had to be recalled from their stations in the Irish Sea. To pay for their hire Loraine signed a cheque for £300. Smart commented, "This operation brought tears to our eyes, for tug-hiring is the most expensive sport I've met." The boats were not used again.

Any likelihood of making the seven mile flight to Holyhead was further diminished next day, August 12th, by a strong wind, gusting up to 40 m.p.h. However, after waiting all day, Loraine's patience ran out and he decided to take a chance. The *Manchester Guardian* reporter described what took place — "all was ready in a very short time. The biplane was on a little slope whence it could get up a good pace to rise. Jules started the engine while Emil and I and half a dozen weird Welsh islanders held the biplane back on the tail. The raising of Loraine's left hand was the signal for us to let go, and away he went. After 50 yards he rose. The islanders yelled with delight; old men and wrinkled women who had driven to the farm and stabled their ponies in the shippons; farm hands, young and strong, with brown faces and Celtic eyes; lads and lasses with bare brown legs; visitors, people in motors, people with bicycles, one and all of this eager crowd shouted and waved as though at their wits end."

But the take-off was downwind. Unable to gain more than 15 feet of height, Loraine was soon in trouble attempting to clear a small hummock. He failed, and badly damaged his aircraft in the ensuing crash, although he himself escaped unhurt.

After this crash it was decided to erect a temporary hangar so that Vedrines could get on with repairs that amounted more or less to a re-build. The spot chosen for this hangar was on lower, flatter ground, a little distance away, near Mynachdy farm. Smart did not like the situation and had a sense of foreboding, which proved in the event to be well founded: it was, "a cup of a place, the centre of a circle of pudding basin hills. It was completely sheltered from the winds and for that reason intensely dangerous and deceptive for flying, for the winds lay over the top of the hollow like a solid lid."

Two problems were immediately apparent — the difficulty of obtaining spare parts, solved by manufacturing them locally at Holyhead marine yards, and Loraine's acting commitments. With only weeks to go before his next production in London, time was critically short. He spent the weekdays rehearsing and then travelled by train to Anglesey for the weekends. There were three clear weekends before acting would demand all his time.

Willing locals soon erected the hangar, but the farmer on whose land the recent events took place, was clearly of a mercenary nature. He presented the following bill;

	£. s. d.
Damage to field by erecting hangar	15.15.0
Damage to field by walking of spectators	5. 5.0
Damage to roads by motor cars	5. 5.0
Damage to fences and gates by people	12. 0.0
Damage to 2 stacks of hay used as beds in hangar	8. 0.0
Damage to field by alighting of aeroplane	2. 0.0
Damage to field by breaking aeroplane	8. 0.0
	£56. 0.0

N.B. — You will pay this before you leave!

Smart reacted with dismay, "There are no roads, no gates, no fences, the aeroplane left no trace when she alighted, but I will have to handle this Methodist farmer carefully, for fear of sabotage." Vedrines also took a strong dislike to the Welsh, as evidenced by his remark, "One knows the English are beasts but here the people are savages!"

Meanwhile he continued to work with great urgency on the task of rebuilding the biplane. After a few days however Smart noticed that the pace was slackening for some reason. It became apparent why this was so when he walked into the hangar one morning and found two women there, who Jules and Emil said were their wives. True or not, the presence of females proved completely disruptive. After threats of dismissal, a strike, and a knife fight between the brothers this potentially disasterous situation was finally resolved by the departure of Emil, his relationship with his brother soured.

Jules returned to work with renewed vigour and by the first weekend of September the Farman was ready to fly once again.

It might be well at this juncture to consider Loraine's flying skills. Though a most enterprising pilot, in truth he was not a good one — there had been too many crashes, constant mishandling, misjudged landings and many narrow escapes. His latest escapade when he was lost over the Irish Sea was a good example. Luck mostly, and the relatively poor performance of early aircraft saved him from paying the ultimate penalty for his errors.

On Sunday September 4th preparations were made for departure. Over the Irish Sea an easterly wind blew whilst at Mynachdy conditions were calm. A large crowd gathered to watch as usual and Vedrines fussed over last minute adjustments. But the flight was doomed before it started. Unfortunately, the field chosen for take off was reclaimed bog which retained much of its boggy characteristics. Hardly had the biplane moved than its wheels sank into the soft ground, the centre section collapsed, pinning Loraine by his legs. Onlookers dragged him from the wreckage and a doctor, who happened to be in the crowd, found the only injuries to his legs were bad bruising and sprains.

The situation now seemed desperate. Only one free weekend remained and the aircraft was in bits for the second time within weeks. Morale sank to rock bottom and there was talk of abandoning the attempt.

Smart, however, urged his friend to continue, knowing the extent of Loraine's ambition. "There's a field at Penrhos Park (Holyhead) — right on the water. Lord Sheffield would let us rig up a hangar there. I'll bring the biplane in by road — Vedrines will fit her up. Anyhow, there'll be no trouble about getting off the ground from there, and once you are off — you'll be right out to sea." His words had the desired effect — there was to be one final effort.

Lord Sheffield did allow a hangar to be put up at Penrhos and the remains of the Farman were taken there by road. In fact this should have happened after the first landing at Bryn Goelcerth. The frustration, extra costs and delays that followed by remaining at Llanfairynghornwy would probably have all been avoided. Indeed, the whole sorry business could have been avoided from the beginning if Loraine, when he took off from Rhos-on-Sea, back in August, had used the lines of the Chester-Holyhead railway to guide him to Holyhead, instead of flying out to sea. The railway line was easy to follow and would have led him unerringly to his destination.

Meanwhile, at Penrhos Vedrines worked at a frantic pace with only a week to complete the job of repairing the Farman. By Sunday the 11th, after the little Frenchman's heroic efforts, everything was ready once more, and in addition, the weather was good — a clear, cold day with a favourable east wind. Loraine had little choice now; he had to make the attempt that day or give up altogether.

The crowd that watched his final preparations was smaller than usual, a few friends and some of Lord Sheffield's staff, servants and tenants of the estate, on their way to church or chapel. Vedrines gave a most prophetic warning, "Be on your guard, it has all been repaired with English wire, I hope it holds." Clearly he thought as little of English wire as he did of English people.

Safety precautions took the form of a cork lifebelt which Loraine wore over his reindeer hair jacket. The advertised (and exaggerated) qualities of this garment included an ability to keep the wearer afloat for five days if necessary. Later, when put to the test, its life saving ability was found to be nil. Indeed it was a positive danger as it very nearly brought about Loraine's death by drowning.

At 11.00 a.m. he climbed into his seat: the engine roared to life and the biplane lifted easily into the air.

Smart and Vedrines waited until the afternoon and then

took the 2.00 p.m. mail boat to Dublin. Half way across they saw another ship, which upon interrogation signalled that a biplane had been seen over the Kish lightship, six miles from Dublin. From this they mistakenly assumed the crossing had been successful and spent the rest of the journey in jubilant mood. Upon arrival in Dublin jubilation turned to mortification when they discovered the truth. Loraine, to his most bitter disappointment, had been forced down into the sea only a few hundred yards from land.

Later, he recounted his experience: "The easterly wind almost doubled my land speed and I was full of buck at having got the flight started — well, just beyond Holyhead Mountain I passed the incoming mail boat, and getting into the line of its wake verified the relative positions of the sun and my compass needle. All the time I was mounting until I must have been 4,000 feet up, and it was a mighty good thing I was too, for without any warning the engine stopped."

The aircraft went into a glide whilst Loraine juggled with the fuel control. Twenty feet above the water, the engine came back to life, enabling height to be regained. Hardly before a reasonable height was reached it stopped again — in fact this happened no less than five times. The fault seemed to be an obstruction in the fuel tank which interupted a constant fuel flow.

"Between whiles I set my course, keeping my eyes glued to the compass on my knee, and feeling a bit desolate. There was nothing to be seen except blue sky and blue sea. No ship did I sight for over 50 minutes, there was nothing to tell me I was steering right except the sun, which only gave me a rough idea.

"Then half way across I ran into a squall of rain which gave me all I could do to keep the machine balanced. I looked at my watch and saw I had been up an hour and grew very nervous. If I was on my right course I must be half way across and I ought to see land.

"But there was nothing, absolutely nothing. I know now

there must have been a lot of haze for all of a sudden I saw a lightship immediately beneath me...I was vastly surprised as I realised it was the Kish and that I had made a dead landfall and the compass had worked splendidly."

Loraine now had only a few miles before reaching the Irish coast. "I can't tell you the exaltation I was in. I looked at my watch and saw it was quarter past twelve. So I had done the 64 miles in an hour and ten minutes, record going for a record crossing — my pulses danced, the blood throbbed in my ears. Then something happened...she began to plunge and dip in the most alarming fashion." The wire used to rig the aircraft was failing. Two control wires broke and made the Farman almost impossible to fly. It lost height rapidly as Loraine struggled to remain airborne, but sadly, at the very last moment, the aircraft plunged into the sea, only a hundred yards from Howth Head. In the water his heavy clothing threatened to pull him down, but eventually he succeeded in swimming to shore. Subsequently, the steamer *"Adela"* salved the biplane, and took it and its crestfallen pilot to Dublin. He said, "When I steamed up the Liffey on this little cargo boat, I could have cried. Here I was grunting into Dublin, when with only two miles more I could have been soaring over it, as I had always dreamed." Nevertheless, it was a fine flight, and a world record for oversea flying. Loraine returned to Holyhead by mail boat that same evening. Two days later he was on the London stage, in a play entitled ironically, "The Man from the Sea." The Royal Aero Club presented him with a silver medal to commemorate the flight, and his theatrical friends gave him a silver statuette representing the marriage of Art and Aviation, embodied in his person.

Following this flight he achieved little of note from an aviation view-point. Vedrines, on the other hand, went on to fulfil his ambition and developed into one of France's leading pilots. He was killed in a flying accident in 1919.

After Loraine, no other pilot showed interest in the Irish Sea crossing until April 1912, when two Irish airmen, R.

Corbett-Wilson and D. Allen decided to race from Hendon to Dublin. It was a somewhat hastily arranged match between friendly rivals, and, in Allen's case, particularly foolish. With only a few months' experience, he had not even undertaken a cross-country flight of any length, let alone an oversea flight.

The plan was to fly by Bradshaw's, (i.e. following railway lines) to Chester, stay overnight and then continue along the coast to Holyhead, and across to Dublin.

At 3.30 p.m. on April 17th the pair took off from Hendon aerodrome in their Bleriot monoplanes and headed north. Allen said later, "I followed the L.N.W.R. line generally, but unfortunately I missed the turning at Crewe!" He eventually arrived at Chester, and landed on the Roodee. There was no sign of Corbett-Wilson. He had abandoned the agreed plan, taking a route via Hereford to Fishguard, from where, on April 22nd he successfully crossed St. George's Channel to Wexford.

Allen meanwhile spent the night at Chester. He was ready to continue at 5 o'clock the next morning but mist delayed his departure until just after six. Safety precautions in case of a ditching were minimal and primitive, consisting of one inflated car wheel tube, later to become a significant pointer to Allen's fate. His last words before taking off were cheerful and confident, "Goodbye, see you in Dublin!"

At half past seven his aircraft was seen flying over Bangor, heading towards Anglesey. Thirty minutes later, observers at Holyhead watched him fly out to sea in calm, bright weather. Allen was never seen again. His mechanic, having arrived at Holyhead during the morning waited in vain for news from Ireland. Fearing the worst, he crossed by the afternoon boat to Dublin, where there was no news whatsoever of Allen. Search parties were organised along the Irish and Welsh coasts, but no trace of the aircraft or its pilot was found. Shipping in the Irish Sea kept a special look-out and a tug left Holyhead to search, but with no results. Then, two weeks later, on May 6th, Irish coastguards at Laytown, near Drogheda, discovered a motor-car tube washed up on the shore, which was identified as the one used by Allen. His fate was a stark reminder of the risks involved, and underlined the fact that flights of this kind could not be embarked upon in a lighthearted manner.

A rather more experienced man, who had been nurturing a desire to attempt the Holyhead-Dublin crossing for some time, without doing much about it, was the Rhyl-based pilot, Vivian Hewitt, already referred to in an earlier section. News of Allen's flight came to him in London, where he was buying spares for his Bleriot. Dismayed at this unexpected event, Hewitt saw his chances diminishing rapidly.

He wrote, "...there was my machine more or less dismantled at Rhyl. I had set my heart so much in wishing to be the first to fly the Irish Sea successfully and here it was being taken out of my hands. I remember saying to my mechanic (Sydney Wingfield) that Allen would be across long before we could get back to Rhyl and have the machine re-assembled and in the air. The only thing which I could do was to complete my purchases of spare parts and wait for news," i.e. whether the flight had been successful or not. When Hewitt saw the headlines "Airman lost in Irish Sea" he wasted no more time. "All that night we raced back in my Targu Floria Bianchi racing car which was fitted with powerful Rushmore headlamps. We arrived at Rhyl early the next morning and with the help of my second mechanic (Arthur Brown) started assembling my Bleriot monoplane. Syd and I were very tired but we kept at it all day. The following day was Saturday and I remember we worked through the whole of that day and far into the night. By 2 a.m. on Sunday morning, 21st April, my machine was ready to take the air. I lay down on some sacks in the hangar and slept for three hours. At 5 a.m. I climbed into the machine and took off." From the moment he became aware of Allen's failure, Hewitt had a constant dread that another pilot might snatch the prize from his grasp. It was this fear that lay behind his tremendous haste. He described his flight thus: "When I reached Llandudno I was flying about 2 miles out to sea at a height of 4,000 feet. As soon as I got round the Great Orme's head I steered straight across approaching Anglesey at its extreme end (Penmon) whence I made for Holyhead Harbour which I could discern in the distance. When I was over Anglesey the wind began to freshen and it got so strong that I experienced great difficulty in guiding my machine." As he flew over the middle of the island the wind became too strong and forced him down, "The machine at times stood perfectly still and I was actually blown backwards across one field. When I eventually landed it was with great difficulty, and I felt very sick as I was being tossed about like a cork." The scene of his forced landing was Plas farm, near Llanerchymedd, where the Bleriot lay for the remainder of that Sunday.

It attracted large crowds of Sabbath-breaking sightseers, its pull clearly strong enough to overcome the strictly imposed Sunday observance of Welsh puritanism. On Monday morning, Hewitt, anxious to continue, decided the wind had abated enough for him to take-off. His aircraft was in a small field and there were stone walls to clear, but a slightly downhill run helped the machine to become airborne. Once in the air, Hewitt realised he had misjudged the weather, as thick haze, and a strong blustering wind made it unsafe to carry on. He flew no further than Holyhead, and landed at Penrhos, on the same spot Loraine used in 1910. During the day he attempted to ascertain weather conditions in the Irish Sea. Captain Newton of the Royal Mail steamer *'Connaught'* arrived in Holyhead at noon and reported heavy mist in the Channel, whilst another mariner, Captain Clay, ex-commodore of the L.N.W.R. steamers, according to the *North Wales Chronicle,* provided Hewitt, "with a chart, a lifebelt, and sound advice!" Strong winds and haze persisted throughout the week, forcing him to wait. Whilst at Holyhead he wrote to *"The Aeroplane,"* then edited by that most strong-minded and formidable man, C. G. Grey.

"You have no doubt heard that I am attempting to cross the Irish Sea. Wilson crossed the St. George's Channel safely and I am up here now waiting for fine weather to do this other crossing..." Grey however, did not think much of this, and wrote in the edition of 25th April, "To Mr. R. Loraine will always belong the honour of being the first man to fly from England to Ireland. Legally and practically he accomplished this feat in September 1910. For not only did he land inside the three-mile limit but actually crossed over the Bailey lighthouse on the end of Howth Head and that the cliffs thereabouts have no beach at the foot on which he could land." This defence of Loraine was probably prompted by Allen's flight earlier in the month, as the magazine would have gone to press by the time Hewitt's letter had been received. For some reason Grey supported Loraine, and wished to convey the idea that the Irish Sea crossing had already been accomplished, but his argument was unconvincing. As William Hywel, Hewitt's biographer remarked, "Surely no race is ever won without breaking the finishing tape... it was never Loraine's intention to crash land in the sea, be he in Irish territorial waters or not."

On Friday the 26th, weather conditions improved sufficiently at Holyhead for Hewitt's flight to take place. He took off from Penrhos at 10.30 a.m., watched by a large crowd, some of whom had been there since 3 a.m. that morning. This departure and the events preceding it were recorded by a cine photographer, whose film was later shown in London cinemas and also some provincial towns, but it is not known if any footage remains extant or not. Hewitt carried no compass and had no accurate information on weather conditions likely to be encountered beyond the local area of Holyhead. His intention was to follow a west nor-west course, navigating it seems by the sun, Captain Clay's chart, and luck.

"When I left Holyhead," he recounted, "the visibility was quite adequate but about half way across the Irish Sea

I ran into a thick bank of fog. I remember thinking at the time this is what must have happened to Leslie Allen. I didn't carry a compass so I had no means of knowing how to navigate, but earlier on I had noticed the angle of the shadow of the sun on my wings. When I got out of the fog I adjusted the course of the plane so that the sun's shadow fell approximately the same as before. It was a great relief when I arrived over land."

Fortunately, the Bleriot's 50 h.p. Gnome engine ran without trouble and Hewitt's navigation had been fairly accurate, having made his landfall some twenty miles south of Dublin. From there it was easy to fly along the coast until, once over the city itself, he could identify his planned landing ground, Phoenix Park. The flight lasted an hour and a quarter and with its successful conclusion Hewitt became the first airman to cross the Irish Sea.

This flight was arguably his finest achievement and boosted his standing as an aviator considerably. For the next two years Hewitt continued to fly, giving many exhibition flights, his reputation much increased, until the outbreak of war in 1914. Then the aerodrome at Voryd was closed and he joined the R.N.V.R., testing Admiralty aircraft at Farnborough. In November 1915 he went to the U.S.A. with the British War Mission and flight-tested many aircraft at the Curtiss plant, Buffalo, N.Y., but after a crash in January 1918 he gave up all flying. Hewitt, having inherited enormous wealth, settled at Cemlyn, on the north west coast of Anglesey, where his peculiarities of character earned him a reputation as an eccentric millionaire. He died in 1965.

Considering the risks and difficulties involved, three of the four aviators who undertook flights over the Irish Sea were remarkably successful and lucky. Corbett-Wilson and Hewitt achieved their objective whilst Loraine failed by a hair's breadth, and only Allen paid the price for his rashness.

Chapter 5

THE FIRST WORLD WAR

The story of aviation in Gwynedd from 1915 to 1918 is bound up exclusively with the fight against German submarines in the Irish Sea. As part of Britain's defence anti-submarine patrols were undertaken by airships and aircraft from a number of bases up and down the country, including two in Gwynedd, one for airships at Llangefni, and another for aircraft at Bangor.

The submarine campaign opened on February 4th, 1915 when Germany announced the coastal waters of Britain and Ireland were regarded as war zones, and every merchant vessel would be sunk. Advocates of all-out war were, however, frustrated as concessions were made, due to American pressure — neutral and hospital ships were to be exempted. One submarine had already penetrated the Irish Sea in January, and sunk three ships off Liverpool. A further two were sunk in the area, probably by the same submarine, during early February.

From the beginning, the Admiralty was aware of the danger and on February 28th a conference was held at which ways and means of meeting the submarine threat were discussed. One idea was to utilise a fleet of small airships which could patrol coastal areas searching for U-boats. They would be operated by the R.N.A.S. (Royal Naval Air Service) from sites near important ports and sea lanes. To provide patrols in the Irish Sea, it was proposed that two stations be established, one at Luce Bay (Wigtown) and another in Anglesey.

But first a suitable type of airship had to be found. No airship was of course immediately available but within weeks of the conference an improvised design had been completed, and the prototype built. It consisted of a

Willows type non-rigid gas envelope attached to a B.E.2C aircraft fuselage. By mid-March the prototype was ready for its first flight, which took place on the 18th and revealed that this hybrid had excellent handling qualities.

A production line was organised without further delay for the airship, by then known as the S.S. (for Submarine Scout, Submarine Spotter or Submarine Searcher — all three appear in various sources). Another unofficial name, which quickly came into general usage was "Blimp." Basil Clarke, *(The History of Airships, 1961)* suggests the following derivation, "Earlier non-rigids had been designated A-limp. Their successors were called B-limp." But there are other explanations also, e.g. an abbreviation of "bloody limp", referring to the frequent state of gas envelopes.

The airship's overall length was 143 feet, with 27 feet beam. Power came from a 70 or 75 h.p. engine giving a cruising speed of about 40 m.p.h. Endurance was eight hours or so, depending on speed, and two crew men were carried — pilot and gunner/wireless operator. Gas capacity was 60,000 cubic feet.

In the meantime, a site for the airship station in Anglesey had been chosen. It was on farm land about three miles from Llangefni, and adjacent to the A5 main road. After requisitioning, work began on the landing ground and buildings. By far the largest building was the airship shed, measuring 40 yards by 106 yards, plus annexes and windshields at either end. The site also included workshops, a gas producing plant, gasholders, and wooden huts to accommodate personnel. By 1916 a whole chain of R.N.A.S. airship stations had been built at Howden (Yorks), Cranwell, Norfolk, London, Kent, Folkestone, Sussex, Cornwall, and Pembroke for instance.

During its four years existence the Anglesey station had a variety of names, ranging from Bodffordd and Gwalchmai (nearby villages) to Llangefni and Heneglwys. The most widely used, officially, seems to have been

Llangefni. It was commissioned on September 26th 1915 as part of No. 14 Group (Naval), with an establishment of four airships, SS22, 24, 25, and 33, the latter fitted with a Maurice Farman fuselage, which had a rear mounted Rolls-Royce 75 h.p. Hawk engine. The others were powered by 70 or 75 h.p. air cooled Renaults.

The station's personnel establishment varied from 130 to 150 men, and its first Commanding Officer was Major George Scott, a leading airship expert who went on to become Deputy Director of Airship Development. Later, Scott lost is life when the R101 crashed at Beauvais, France in 1930. R.N.A.S. Llangefni's task was two-fold. Firstly to escort shipping in the Irish Sea, particularly vessels bound for Liverpool; and the Holyhead-Dublin traffic, thereby affording some measure of protection against the threat of submarine attack, and secondly, to carry out regular patrols. This meant long hours of flying, ranging far and wide over the sea, keeping a constant look-out.

In the event of a submarine actually being found, the airships had little chance of making a successful attack, armed as they were with only a Lewis gun, a few small bombs and no proper bomb sights. Nor were they meant to; their primary function was to relay details, such as position etc. to Royal Navy surface vessels, who were far better equipped to make an attack. The Irish Sea surface patrol vessels were based at Holyhead, and consisted of motor launches, armed yachts and trawlers. Later, when America entered the war, they were strengthened by U.S. Navy destroyers and launches.

Obviously, rapid communication between airship, base, and surface vessel was of paramount importance and to this end, a new technology, used for the first time in war, was employed — wireless. In September 1915 the Admiralty approved a scheme to build special wireless stations for airship communications. There were two types: the 'X' station, transmitting and receiving messages, and the 'B' station, which transmitted a directional signal only, as an aid to position finding.

Two of these stations were built in North Wales, by the Marconi Co. — an 'X' type at Amlwch, to serve R.N.A.S. Llangefni, and a 'B' type at Rhyl. Both were in use by March 1916. However, the wireless equipment installed in airships was relatively primitive and subject to frequent breakdown.

The job of providing anti-submarine patrols could not be described as glamorous or particularly exciting. On the contrary, it necessitated spending long, exhausting hours scanning the sea in a never-ending search for a submarine's presence, through such tell-tale signs as periscope wake, and oil patches. In addition, the mere presence of an airship would force an U-boat commander to keep his head down, as it were, and hinder his freedom to look for targets.

Sir Walter Raleigh, the military historian, likened this work to fishing — "The flying officer who patrols on the look-out for underwater craft must have the patience, watchfulness and ability of the angler. Submarine hunting has been described as a serious sport in which the fish are not at all keen to rise to the fly."

The Anglesey airships flew every day on their patrol and escort duty, except in very strong winds. Their sector extended roughly from Bardsey Island, to Dublin, up to the Isle of Man and Morecombe Bay. Most patrols were carried out at heights ranging from a few hundred to 1,000 feet. The pilots had to combine flying skills with observation, navigation, and when necessary, bomb-aiming. Luckily, the first months of R.N.A.S. Llangefni's existence, a 'settling down' period coincided with a lull, during the winter of 1915-16, in U-boat activity.

This was due to the unresolved argument amongst German military commanders, whether to pursue unrestricted submarine war or not. A desire to blockade Britain using U-boats was countered by the fear of possible American involvement, and its undoubted boost to the Allied war effort. In March 1916, a compromise was reached — enemy freighters in the war zone were to be torpedoed, those outside it were to be attacked only if armed. Passenger steamers were to be left strictly alone. Though four U-boats were in Irish waters by March, many vessels were allowed to proceed unhindered — because of these restrictions.

Meanwhile the airships continued their ceaseless daily patrols. Some officers, frustrated by lack of action, complained they were merely animated scarecrows. There was some truth in this, but nevertheless, the job remained a useful and important one.

Of course, it was not all routine patrolling. One popular activity, which provided some entertainment and friendly competition was bombing and machine gunning practice. For this purpose a submarine shaped target had been laid out in a corner of the landing ground, and small 16 lb. bombs dropped on it. But equipment was primitive to say the least — bombs hung on a string and two crossed nails serving as a bombsight.

Generally, the airships were reliable to operate. Most trouble came from the engines — 70 or 75 h.p. air-cooled Renaults, with a tendency to overheat. They were designed for aircraft, with higher speeds (and therefore more efficient cooling) than the SS's gentle 40-45 m.p.h.

The safety record of airships at Anglesey was good also. Many small mishaps occurred, but serious accidents were rare and fatal ones rarer still — only one in 1916, when SS18, then based at Llangefni, was lost on November 9th. Whilst attempting to land it struck a cow, killing the unfortunate animal and damaging the control car. When the wireless operator decided to jump out of his cockpit, the airship, suddenly lightened, rose upwards out of control. In these circumstances it took on the characteristics of a free balloon, going wherever the wind took it. For some reason, gas was not, or could not be, released in order to lose height.

Eventually SS18 was blown out to sea, where its pilot, Sub. Lt. A. Thompson managed to valve gas, bringing the airship down quickly. It fell heavily into the sea and the engineer then jumped, or was thrown out by the impact. Either way, this caused the airship once more to rise, now with only its pilot on board. Finally, it came down with such violence that the envelope and car were broken in two. Thompson clung to wreckage until rescued by a passing steamer, but the engineer drowned.

Forced landings on Anglesey itself happened sometimes, usually because of rough running or failed engines. These were events that gave some of the island's good people a totally novel, and at times, frightening experience — that of airship handling. When faced with the possibility of drifting or a forced landing after engine failure, the airship's crew would let down grapnels and trail ropes, in an attempt to bring their craft under control. Any onlookers below would be urgently invited to "catch hold of the ropes" (a phrase vividly remembered by those who heard it), but most that heeded the command were simple, country people, and totally ignorant of airship handling. More than one, having grabbed a rope, found himself dragged along the ground, or worse still, lifted a few feet into the air.

Many disregarded the request to "catch hold of the ropes" altogether, not because they were unhelpful, or indifferent to the plight of others, but simply because they did not understand English. In the small, tight-knit rural communities of the island, Welsh was the only language spoken, and to their inhabitants the airship crew were almost foreigners.

Probably, of the Anglesey populance, Llangefni residents got to know the R.N.A.S. men best. The C.O., Major Scott stayed at the Bull Hotel, and most of his officers and ratings also used the town as a focus of social activity. Their capacity for drinking and boisterous behaviour quickly became legend, and an appearance before the local magistrates was not at all uncommon.

In 1917 things began to change. Increased activity in the Irish Sea, both on the surface and below it, put considerable pressure on the airships and their ability to carry out effective patrols.

On January 15th orders were issued to U-boat commanders to operate without limitations, to sink ships on sight and without warning. It was to be a final supreme effort to cut off Britain's supply lines completely.

The unrestricted campaign was to begin on February 1st, in the certain knowledge it would bring America into the war. Three days later the Americans broke off diplomatic relations with Germany, and on April 5th declared war. The Germans lost no time in the Irish Sea, sinking six vessels near Bardsey in the second week of February.

An extra duty for the airships after May 1917 was the provision of escorts for convoys (introduced that month) bound for Liverpool. They were well-suited to the task, with long endurance and an ability to adjust their speed to that of the convoy.

Also during this period efforts to combat the submarine menace took another step forward when successful experiments with hydrophones were carried out. These were basically underwater microphones, lowered from an airship into the sea, to detect sounds from any submerged submarines in the vicinity. A number of R.N.A.S. stations took part in the experiments, including Llangefni. The C.O. wrote to the Admiralty on May 19th:-

"I have to report that I carried out the following experiments with a hydrophone on 18th May 1917. The hydrophone was suspended 180 feet below the airship and towed through the sea at a depth of 5 fathoms at a speed of 10 knots. The experiment was carried out in conjunction with M.L.221 under very unfavourable weather conditions. The propellor of the Motor Launch was heard very distinctly at a range of 1 mile. Signals were given to the Motor Launch, "Stop", "Slow" and "Full Ahead" in order to detect the difference in sound and most valuable information was received. After a time the hydrophone vane broke off and caused it to become unstable — but even with this drawback results were obtained.

The shape of the hydrophone is unsuitable for towing and in future should be shaped like an aerial bomb.

Further experiments are being carried out with an improved shape of hydrophone and a new type of cable and winding gear. A Motor Launch or submarine could be heard at a range of at least 3 miles. Hydrophones could be used with valuable results in airships searching for submarines as an airship can 'hover' or go 'dead slow' over the sea, thereby decreasing the "sing" of the microphone. Should this experiment meet your approval it is requested a consignment of 1,000 feet of steel cable may be supplied.

signed: Squadron Commander
A.Corbett-Wilson, C.O."
(no relation to the Corbett-Wilson mentioned
in the previous chapter)

The Admiralty's Director of Air Services replied that he was gratified to receive these results, which he regarded as most promising. Hydrophone experiments continued into 1918, when the Admiralty authorised their installation in airships, but the war ended before they came into general use.

Other experiments made by the Anglesey airships included the use of phosphorous, on sea water, as a means of creating smoke screens, and some very unpopular trials in which engines were run on hydrogen. With a suitably modified carburetor, hydrogen could be drawn directly from the airship's gas bags, during the final stages of a flight for instance, when loss of gas was of no importance. It seemed to offer the possibility of reduced petrol consumption.

The result was similar in all trials — a rough running engine and an extremely apprehensive crew. Much relief greeted the Admiralty's signal ordering these experiments to cease. The month of June 1917 saw a major change with the introduction of an improved, 'Mark II', SS airship.

Known as SSPs (for Pusher) they had increased beam, giving a gas volume of 70,000 cubic feet, whilst the control car had been developed from the Maurice Farman aircraft fuselage. Three crew members were carried in tandem, gunner/wireless operator, pilot, and engineer, whose responsibility was a rear mounted, water-cooled Green engine. In service these engines proved unreliable and a constant source of trouble.

Only six SSPs were built, three of which, SSP1, 5, and 6 ended up at Llangefni replacing SS22, 24 and 33 which had given faithful service since September 1915.

Llangefni's crews had to familiarise themselves with the new airships during a busy period when heavy demands were already being made on their patrolling capacity. In addition, they had to instruct unqualified pilots sent to meet a shortage of personnel at the station. In order to bring them up to standard, extra instructional flights had to be provided, but whenever circumstances allowed, such flights were combined with actual patrols and escorts.

Another development during the summer of 1917 was the establishment of a mooring-out station near Dublin. It had become apparent that an airship station was needed on the eastern Irish coast. The airships from Anglesey spent much time in that area, whilst escorting mail and troop ships to and from Dublin, for instance, and a small station near the city would relieve the pressure on Anglesey considerably. A shed capable of holding two airships was thought suitable.

Admiralty approval was given on June 7th, and so a landing ground and airship shed were built in the grounds of Malahide Castle, just north of Dublin. Malahide mooring-out station proved to be a very useful additional facility and worked well in conjunction with Anglesey.

A marked difference however was the hostility of local people. Whereas Welsh people were generally welcoming, or at worst, indifferent, in Ireland there was openly expressed resentment of an English presence. The Easter rising of 1916, and its repression was fresh in the minds of many Irishmen.

An R.N.A.S. officer records the extent of this animosity — "We had no telephone at Malahide at first and had to go to the local police station for messages. When returning on one occasion in the sidecar of a motor cycle, our only ground transport at the time, our speed was increased by a hail of bullets, which fortunately did us no damage. Some time after that our ancient Ford, running with supplies from Dublin was waylaid with a rope across the road. Both the driver and the van were damaged but not irreparably."

During the late summer and autumn of 1917, U-boat activity in the Irish Sea increased, from an already high level, putting considerable pressure on all anti-submarine forces, including airship patrols. This situation arose due to the convoy systems' success in drastically reducing shipping losses in the Atlantic and Western Approaches.

Submarine commanders, deprived of targets in these areas, were forced to step up operations in British coastal waters, where ships, large and small could still be found, sailing alone and independently. From this time until the war ended, a number of U-boats, active in the Irish Sea and Liverpool Bay, were responsible, despite frequent anti-submarine patrols, for sinking many ships. Amongst them, the *Eskmere* (2,300 tons), sunk 15 miles off South Stack in September; the *Adada* (7,800 tons), sunk three miles off Point Lynas in November, with 77 lives lost; and the *Earl of Elgin* (4,400 tons) in Caernarfon Bay, plus other, smaller vessels.

This of course placed a great burden on the airship crews at Llangefni in their attempts to provide as many escorts and patrols as possible. During October the work load became so heavy that a request for assistance was sent to the Admiralty. In response came a message stating that six D.H.4 aircraft would be sent to assist.

They took off on the morning of November 7th, 1917 from a Midlands base (unfortunately the record does not state exactly where but it could well be Castle Bromwich).

As soon as the aircraft approached North Wales they encountered bad weather.

Only two machines reached Gwynedd, where strong winds, rain and mist made flying hazardous. One pilot decided to give up near Aber when he saw the temptingly broad expanse of Traeth Lafan (Lavan Sands) exposed by low tide. He made a successful landing.

The other pilot, 2nd Lt. Bernard Carter RFC, continued until he eventually succeeded in locating Llangefni. Sadly however, this feat of airmanship and navigation ended in disaster when he crashed attempting to land. Eye-witnesses thought the aircraft (A7654) had been caught by a strong gust of wind whilst making a steep turn, or equally, it could have been stalled by a tired pilot who relaxed his concentration too soon after a difficult flight. However the accident happened, 2nd Lt. Carter was killed, and his observer, Corporal Harold Smith, badly injured. It was the first fatal flying accident in Gwynedd.

Meanwhile back on Lavan Sands, the pilot and observer of the other D.H.4 were anxiously trying to salvage their aircraft from the wet sand. Help was sought from a local farmer who took his horses out to the machine. Progress was slow — too slow in fact, as an incoming tide put an end to the attempt. Men and horses were forced to retreat, leaving the aircraft to its fate. Eventually after a few days, the engine was successfully salvaged and what remained of the fuselage set on fire.

At this point it is worth mentioning what is, at the time of writing, a mystery. According to a local diarist of the period, Jane Adeane of Holyhead, on the day after Lt. Carter's death, another fatal accident occurred. She wrote on November 9th —

> "An airship fell a few miles from here in Anglesey. Two young men of 20 were killed on the spot; another recovered his senses enough to say they had flown from Lincolnshire and were on their way to Ireland, and added "Take out the bombs at once

before they explode." As nothing is allowed in the papers, this accident will perhaps not be attended to. It is believed they were wanted for Ireland."

The problem arising out of this account is the lack of verifying references which can be found in official records. There seems to be no record of an airship lost in Anglesey on that date and furthermore, no reference to such an accident is made by Captain T. B. Williams in his book 'Airship Pilot No. 28', which recounts his experiences as an airship pilot in Anglesey at the time these events were supposed to have occurred. Captain Williams relates his story in great detail, including the accident that befell Lt. Carter but does not mention a second accident on the following day. Could it be that Mrs. Adeane was simply misinformed about the circumstances of Lt. Carter's death?

Whilst R.N.A.S. Llangefni struggled to provide the maximum number of escorts and patrols, submarine attacks continued unabated. In December nine vessels were sunk off Anglesey, and during the first quarter of 1918 another twenty ships suffered a similar fate, with the loss of fifty six lives. There could be no doubt that the maximum effort made by German submarines was providing a major headache both for the local R.N. Commander at Holyhead Naval Base (with whom Llangefni cooperated closely of course) and the Admiralty's higher echelons.

Strengthening of anti-submarine measures became an urgent requirement, not only in the Irish Sea, but other important sea areas around Britain, such as the North Sea and English Channel. Changes brought about by the Admiralty in response to this crisis included further development of the basic SS airship design and introduction of aircraft patrols to supplement those already being carried out by airships.

These patrols were to operate within a few miles of the coast only, as 60% of sinkings were taking place ten miles or less from shore. This would free airships to provide escort cover further from land, where their superior endurance could be used to advantage.

Design of the new airship began early in 1918. Known as the SSZ (for Zero), it incorporated improvements over previous airships which, in service, made it a firm favourite with crews. Gas capacity remained unchanged from the SSPs, but the boat-shaped control car, unlike its predecessors, was specifically designed for airship use. It also proved to have an excellent floating capability.

Other features included extra room for the three man crew, improved visibility and a greater arc of fire for the Lewis gun. Bomb racks were fitted, and the bomb load increased to 300 lbs (either three 100 lbs. bombs or one 230 lbs plus one 100 lbs) — still inadequate to attack a submarine with any hope of success, but the SSZs' prime role remained as before — provision of patrol and escort duty only. Power came from a rear-mounted Rolls Royce 75 h.p. Hawk engine. Endurance varied according to speed — e.g. 16 hours at 50 m.p.h., or 40 hours at 20 m.p.h.

In March and early April the SSPs were withdrawn from service at Llangefni. Two, SSP1 and 6 (recently repaired after being badly damaged in a forced landing near Blackburn due to engine failure) were taken over by Cranwell for training purposes. They were replaced by four Zeros, SSZ 34, 35, 50 and 51, plus SSZ 72 and 73 which were based at Malahide mooring out station.

The capacity to float was used to advantage during SSZ35s' very first patrol, on April 8th — a 7½ hour stint in Liverpool Bay. Returning to Llangefni Z35's crew brought her down near a fishing boat and did some business. In a few minutes they were airborne again with fresh fish for tea!

Meanwhile, plans to introduce aircraft patrols in the Irish Sea continued as part of a much larger general scheme which forsaw the establishment of twenty nine coastal patrol flights, mainly on the eastern side of the country.

On March 14th, 1918, Squadron Commander Allsop visited Llangefni, and in company with the station's C.O., Squadron Commander Brotherton, undertook a survey of possible landing sites. A number were located in Anglesey, but rejected as being too marshy, having bad approaches, or requiring too much labour to prepare.

The airship station itself, which seemed the most logical place, was deemed unsuitable because too much work was necessary to bring its generally rough ground up to standard.

An Admiralty policy document set out the purpose, and limitations of these intended patrols — "The submarine will not be willing to remain on the surface or to operate with its periscope showing while any aeroplane is in sight...the work of the submarine as regards torpedo and gun fire attack is prevented as long as aircraft is (sic) in sight... While obviously it would be best to use fast machines armed with heavy bombs and manned by skilled pilots and observers yet even slow and obsolete machines carrying a pilot and without any bombs at all are better than nothing, they will prevent the submarine from operating. The primary object in protected lanes is not so much to destroy the submarines, which is a matter of great skill and practice, but to frighten them off, which is easy." In other words, aircraft, like airships were to be "animated scarecrows."

Slow and obselete machines, suggested in the report, were available in quantity. During February 1918 some 300 D.H.6 trainers became surplus to requirements. They were simple, even crude, aircraft of poor performance, superseded by the Avro 504.

Not only were the aircraft second rate, but their pilots also. The Admiralty envisaged, "A fair number of low grade pilots could be made available at once for the proposed service," by which they meant training school failures, survivors from the Western Front, and even those with physical disabilities, who would otherwise have been barred from any kind of flying.

Whilst these plans were taking shape, the Royal Air Force came into being formally on April 1st, together with a new government department, the Air Ministry. Those at R.N.A.S. Llangefni found themselves transferred to the R.A.F. overnight, although organisational responsibility for the station remained in Admiralty hands.

Responsibility for aircraft patrols now fell to the R.A.F. One immediate, unresolved question was the siting of a landing ground. Squadron Commander Allsop's suggestions for sites in Anglesey had all been rejected in March, but the search for others continued. Eventually a coastal site was found between Bangor and the village of Aber, where a narrow strip of flat land separates the sea from Snowdonia's mountains.

Fifty acres of this land, constituting a sizeable part of Glanmor Isa Farm was requisitioned in May. For the farmer it was an unexpected and unpleasant surprise. Indeed, losing the use of so much land caused him considerable hardship during the next twelve months. But winning the battle against predatory U-boats was of over-riding importance. Nine ships had already been sunk in the Irish Sea during April.

On the 26th, a submarine was reported in Liverpool Bay, where SSZ35 happened to be patrolling. She immediately joined in the search but near Formby lighthouse her engine failed, much to the crew's chagrin, just after a message was received stating the submarine had been sighted. After drifting helplessly for a while, Z35 was taken in tow by a trawler, eventually to be deposited after losing most of her gas, on the beach at Llandudno.

Quickly a large crowd gathered, whilst the airship was tied down safely alongside the Hydro Hotel to await the arrival of a repair party from Anglesey. Meantime Z35's pilot, Fl. Lt. T. B. Williams was having dinner at the Hydro, by kind invitation of the Management!

On the following day, engine failure occurred again despite a thorough overhaul. It happened minutes after taking-off on a test flight. The pilot's report is quoted in full, plus a contemporary eye-witness recollection, as they illustrate some of the problems of airship handling, seen from a professional viewpoint, and from that of local people.

Flt. Lt. Williams wrote — "On 27-4-18 SSZ 35 left ground at 1805 for engine trials, wind NE 14-16 mph. Engine seized 10 minutes after leaving ground. Ship drifted over station at 800 feet. Gas was valved and grapnel dropped when suitable position reached, about 3 miles from Station. Grapnel caught in a hedge and ship swung violently sideways and downwards. When a few feet above the ground, passenger (the Station Engineer Officer) was instructed to jump out and prevent grapnel coming adrift if possible. This was accomplished with the aid of a woman from a nearby cottage. On the arrival of a number of civilians, ship was hauled down and farm labourers instructed how to keep her "nose to wind" by aid of the handling guys. Soon afterwards a party arrived from the Station. It was found possible a little later to run engine sufficiently to blow up ship to pressure. Ship was then let up on a trail rope and walked across country back to the shed."

In fact Z35 came down near the hamlet of Cerrigeinwen, where one man recalled the event nearly sixty five years after it took place. Then only a young boy, he clearly remembers his mother grabbing a rope hanging from the airship which to his horror, lifted her a few feet off the ground before she released the rope.

He also recounted the story of Z35's return journey to Llangefni. The narrow country roads could not be used due to hazards such as trees. Instead, a cross country route had to be taken, avoiding all obstacles. However, none of the R.N.A.S. men possessed sufficient knowledge of local geography to select a safe route. Clearly, a local person was needed, someone with good knowledge of all fields and woods.

From the group clinging to Z35's trail ropes one man volunteered — Hugh Parry of Cerrig Engan Farm. Well known as something of a 'character' in the district, and fond of a drink or two, Parry knew of the R.N.A.S.'s similar propensities, and thought a few free pints of beer, at the very least, would be his reward.

Slowly, and with great care, the airship was taken by a long tortuous route, under Hugh Parry's guidance until, eventually, the party arrived back at the landing ground. Once Z35 was safely moored, civilian helpers were curtly dismissed with bare thanks. Hugh Parry and friends departed throwing Welsh oaths at all airships and the mean devils who flew them!

Another story, perhaps worth relating here, tells of a local man, rather eccentric but harmless, who, with delusions of grandeur, managed to obtain, somehow, a high ranking naval officer's uniform — reputed to be an admiral's. As befitted his status he decided to give the Station a surprise inspection. Apparently his unexpected arrival caused momentary panic, but the deception could not be sustained for long. Once the truth was revealed the 'admiral's' inspection came to a sudden end. He continued to wear his uniform however, and was said to have been amongst the leaders of the Victory Parade at Holyhead in 1918!

But to return to more serious aspects of the war — as part of the general strengthening of Irish Sea anti-submarine activities — Captain Gordon Campbell V.C. was appointed in March 1918 to command and co-ordinate all sea and air forces engaged in the fight.

Based at Holyhead, Campbell commanded, as he put it, "A flotilla of old destroyers, a yacht, a drifter, about twenty motor launches, four airships, and a squadron of aeroplanes." A forceful, decisive man, he earned his V.C. for sinking three U-boats as captain of a "Q" ship (an armed ship disguised as a defenceless merchantman) and was the ideal choice for the job of "clearing up the Irish Sea", to use his phrase.

In June the 'squadron of aeroplanes' mentioned by Campbell arrived at Glanmor Isa Farm. It was not a full squadron, but rather two flights of 255 Squadron, newly formed for coastal patrol duties. Four other flights were also formed, two at Pembroke and two at Luce Bay, all within the control of 77 Wing, No. 14 Group.

In fact a number of new squadrons were formed, all in the 250 series, to carry out anti-submarine coastal patrols. Most were on the north east coast of England between Hull and Newcastle, where they patrolled the North Sea area.

Little preparation had been necessary for the aircrafts' arrival at Glanmor Isa, just the uprooting of a few hedges and erection of four Bessoneau hangars. Officers and men lived in tents, suitably separated of course. Stores of fuel and bombs were sited between two small woods — the bombs kept in trenches, covered only by tarpaulin. It was not the best method of storage by any means and caused, in general, many defective ones. But the wireless section at least, had a roof over its head, in one of the farm outbuildings.

Unfortunately it is difficult to piece together the detailed history of this small R.A.F. encampment because so few sources are available. No squadron operations' record book, for example, exists. Such a source would provide an invaluable record of day to day flying activity, but the makeshift conditions under which the camp was set up, and its impermanence seemed to preclude record keeping. Only a very broad view of events can be given.

During August 1918 some general re-organisation of the coastal patrol squadrons took place, as a result of which 255's two flights at Glanmor Isa were joined by a third and the unit re-numbered 244 Squadron. At first the three flights were simply named A, B, and C but following further changes all flights within the 'Scarecrow' (if they can be called by this apt but unflattering name) Squadrons were allocated numbers — 244's three becoming 521, 522, and 530 Flights, with an establishment of eighteen aircraft, all D.H.6s.

They were responsible for patrolling coastal shipping

lanes, extending from Anglesey to Liverpool Bay. These lanes were constantly patrolled, each patrol lasting on average 1½ hours. One disadvantage of the D.H.6 when used for this duty was its inability to carry anything resembling a reasonable bomb load. Some aircraft were therefore flown as single seaters, with the observer replaced by bombs ranging from 65lbs to 230lbs. Others flew as twin seaters, with an observer, but no bombs, and were used particularly for convoy escort work. Generally the proportion was 75% single seaters and 25% twin seaters.

In September the squadron suffered a fatal accident when one of the D.H.6s crashed immediately after taking off. Its injured pilot, Captain Tuck, and observer, Air Mechanic W. Shaw were taken to hospital at Bangor, where Air Mechanic Shaw died soon after. This seems to have been the most serious accident, but many other mishaps occurred, such as forced landings and ditchings. Luckily the D.H.6 had excellent floating characteristics.

During the summer a report on the employment of aircraft for anti-submarine work was prepared by the CO of 18 Group, R.A.F. — Col. Williamson — for the Admiralty. He concluded that aircraft had superiority over airships where constant flying close to the coast was required; patrol and escort could be provided in almost all weathers, particularly when strong winds were blowing and thereby keeping the airships grounded.

He continued, "The proportion of serious accidents is not great. On numerous occasions machines have descended in the sea, ..., but nevertheless no lives have been lost." A pencilled note in the report's margin corrects this with 'one from Anglesea', but whether this refers to Captain Tuck's accident, or Lt. Carter at Llangefni in 1917, or another accident, is not known.

Colonel Williamson concluded his report with an appreciation of the problems faced by coastal patrol flights — "... considerable credit is due to pilots who first undertook the anti-submarine work, flying land machines over the sea, particularly the D.H.6, a training machine of poor performance and by no means well suited to this class of work. It is to be remembered that these flights had to start work under difficult conditions, in squadrons hastily organised with personnel under canvas, no repair facilities and in all cases a serious shortage of non-commissioned airmen in the technical grades."

Armourers for instance were usually not available and Flights were constantly short of mechanics. It was not surprising that bombs were so unreliable, (moreover, the D.H.6 had no proper bombsight) and that aircraft serviceability problems arose. For example, in early October 244 Squadron had seventeen aircraft serviceable, but the number fell steadily to twelve, and at one point in November it was down to just five aircraft, but by mid-December was back to seventeen.

Just before the Armistice in November, 530 Flight moved to Tallaght, near Dublin, in order to provide local patrols. However, the Armistice put an end to these patrols, and one month later the Flight was absorbed back into its parent squadron at Glanmor Isa.

When winter came the squadron's tented accommodation, barely adequate in summer, now became totally inadequate. Heavy rain, flooding, high winds and cold made life under canvas extremely uncomfortable. The problem was solved by billetting at Penrhyn Castle, the home of Lord Penrhyn, about one mile away.

Winter gales also blew down two of the hangars and overturned some aircraft. Rain caused waterlogging of the flying ground frequently. Early in 1919 it became totally unusable, but by then so little flying took place that it did not matter overmuch.

Meanwhile the airships of R.N.A.S. Llangefni were also busy during the summer and autumn months of 1918 providing escorts and patrols in the Irish Sea. On May 9th for example the log shows all four airships operating:-
SSZ34   — patrolled northern and western coast of Anglesey — 10 hours and 45 minutes

SSZ35	— patrolled Liverpool Bay trade route and escorted troopship from Holyhead to Kingstown
SSZ50	— patrolled Liverpool Bay trade route, 4 hours 50 minutes, returned to base with engine trouble
SSZ51	— escorted troopship from Holyhead to Kingstown and escorted mail ship back to Holyhead — 7 hours 45 minutes

In fact May turned out to be a good month for the airships when, on the 18th, SSZ50 located a submarine near the Skerries. A stream of oil forming on the water, and moving in a westerly direction, gave clear indication that a submarine was underneath the surface. Dropping a 100lb. bomb from a low height had no effect. Height was then gained to increase the effectiveness of the next bomb, a 230 pounder, which produced an underwater explosion of some force. Meantime, messages had been passed to two other airships patrolling near Bardsey, and Royal Navy surface vessels of the Irish Sea Flotilla, from which a destroyer was sent to attack the submarine. But the result was inconclusive although it was certain that some damage had been inflicted.

Before dawn on the following day, three airships were out again patrolling with extra vigilance. At four thirty a.m., SSZ51, positioned 12 miles south west of Bardsey Island saw the periscope wake and dark shadow of a submarine hull travelling in a south-westerly direction. Messages were sent, giving the submarine's position and a 230 lb. bomb dropped.

Soon, SSZ35, who was not far, joined in the attack. Another 230 lb. bomb was dropped, but with no effect. Then, four destroyers — three American, one British — arrived and began dropping depth charges, which, in the words of one airship pilot, "knocked the bottom out of the sea."

Following this attack, oil, air bubbles, and debris appeared on the water in large quantities, confirming that the submarine had been destroyed. Subsequent research has identified it as U-B.119, which left Germany on April 27th for the Irish Sea. Most probably it was the same submarine attacked, and damaged on the previous day.

But other submarines remained active during May it seems judging from these log extracts:

27th SSZ34 — patrolled Caernarfon Bay, 10 hours 15 minutes, dropped 230 lb. bomb on rising bubbles of oil, position 53.3N, 4.45W (result unknown)

SSZ50 — patrolled (with destroyer) N.W. to W. of Holyhead and Caernarfon Bay trade routes. 12 hours, 15 minutes. Searched for submarine reported in position 53.3N and 5.28W.

SSZ51 — patrolled (with destroyer) area West of Caernarfon Bay and Bardsey — 16 hours. Dropped 230 lb. bomb on large bubbles of oil (result unknown)

29th SSZ34 — worked with destroyer searching for reported submarine.

No further U-Boats were actually located and attacked by the airships however.

Towards the end of June 1918, a spell of good weather allowed two R.N.A.S. pilots, Fl. Lts. Williams and Farina, to embark on a flight, planned for some time, by which they hoped to set up the endurance record for an SSZ airship. At dawn on the 29th they left Llangefni in Z35 with Air Mechanic Rawlins as wireless operator.

Flying very slowly to minimise fuel consumption and thereby maximise endurance, a circuitous route took them to Northern Ireland, across to Scotland, down to the Isle of Man, then eastwards to Blackpool, before turning for Liverpool. From there they continued along the North Wales coast to Holyhead, then Z35 headed south across Caernarfon Bay and the west coast of Wales.

After 24 hours of this, all three, not surprisingly felt tired and bored. They decided to make for base.

When crossing the Anglesey coast, a small bomb was

dropped by Fl. Lt. Farina on an offshore rock, just as a diversion. But as Z35 was flying low and travelling at minimum speed, it was too close to the bomb when it exploded. A splinter punctured the envelope, allowing gas to escape. The previous snail's pace suddenly turned into a quick sprint before loss of gas made a forced landing inevitable! This turn of speed made little difference to the flight's outcome — an endurance record of twenty six hours and ten minutes. Williams and Farina discovered afterwards Z35's petrol gauge was faulty — half the fuel remained unused. Later, the record was raised to 56 hours and 55 minutes by Captain Bryan, AFC, in SSZ 39.

As already mentioned, U-boat attacks were on the decrease throughout the summer, but isolated sinkings still took place. In August the *'Boscawen'* was sunk between Holyhead and Bardsey, whilst the *Snowdon* managed to survive being torpedoed when sailing from Holyhead to Dublin.

The final sinking was on October 10th, when the mail boat *'Leinster'* was torpedoed with heavy loss of life. Bad weather that day kept Llangefni's airships grounded, otherwise the loss might have been avoided.

On October 21st, all U-boats at sea were recalled by the German Admiralty, thus bringing the campaign against Allied shipping to an end. For Germany it had been a failure: Britain's maritime supply lines were not cut and the war was now clearly lost, on all fronts. However, the war fought by U-boats revealed what a formidable weapon the submarine could be with full use of its capabilities.

The war finally ended with the signing of the Armistice on November 11th. News of the signing reached Holyhead at 6.00 a.m. that morning when a wireless operator at the naval base, whilst monitoring transmissions, intercepted a radio broadcast from Paris — "Hostilities will cease on all fronts at eleven o'clock." Although not 'official' the news spread like wildfire.

At 9.00 a.m. the airships of RNAS Llangefni flew to

Holyhead where they dropped bombs in the sea, as a prelude to the celebrations to follow.

Also at 9.00 a.m. proclamatory posters appeared in the windows of the *North Wales Chronicle,* at Bangor. The paper described what followed:-

"Shortly afterwards one of the RAF motor lorries from Aber rumbled up the High Street, filled with airmen, who vociferously chorused the great news to the staccato accompaniment of a raucous hooter. Flags appeared all over the place... The airmen from Aber apparently forgetting that Bangor was out of bounds for them owing to the flu epidemic, came in their motor lorries, into which a large proportion of the small boys of the town mysteriously found their way.

After lunchtime a procession was formed by the airmen, many of whom were fantastically garbed... But the outstanding feature of the afternoon was an aerial performance. First came two airships and as they majestically flew over Bangor their silvery covers glistening in the sunshine, they presented a magnificent spectacle. Flying at very low altitude the occupants waved their hats to the crowd in the High Street. Then two aeroplanes in charge of skilful pilots performed 'stunts' which made the crowd fairly gasp, especially when one of them looped the loop rather close to the roofs."

Shortly after the Armistice, Captain Campbell, who had been responsible for succesfully co-ordinating all anti-submarine activity in the Irish Sea, held a number of parties, including one for the airship and aircraft pilots. At this party were the two Commanding Officers, Major Elmhurst of the R.N.A.S. and Major Probyn of the R.A.F.

Probyn had given Captain Campbell a flight in one of the squadron's D.H.6s, ending in a run under the Menai Bridge. Jokingly he challenged Major Elmhurst to do the same in an airship. The challenge was immediately accepted, but first official permission had to be given — by Campbell. He admitted it was a foolish idea, but the

Armistice spirit was upon them, and he agreed provided that he was one of the crew!

A few days later, Elmhurst, Campbell and Air Mechanic Charles Jones (a local man as it happened) headed for the Menai Straits. The plan was to fly their airship just a few feet above the water with the aid of a specially marked lead line. This would ensure maximum clearance for the airship (overall height 45 feet) under the bridge's 150 foot high span. Approaching from the north east, or Bangor side, Elmhurst took his airship smoothly and without any trouble under the Menai Bridge, much to the amazement of onlookers and possibly the crew also. Could this have been the only occasion when an airship flew underneath a bridge?

Once the war ended there was little for the SSZeros of Llangefni and 244's D.H.6s to do. The reason for their existence had gone with the disappearance of U-boats from the Irish Sea. On November 22nd, Malahide mooring out station closed and 530 Flight was recalled from Tallaght in December, whilst the parent stations went on a 'care and maintenance' basis until the Admiralty and Air Ministry decided on their future.

For 244 Squadron, clearly there was no future and disbandment was inevitable. The official date was January 22nd 1919, although some of the airmen remained for a few weeks, carrying out work for the Penrhyn estate. By May, the Air Ministry decided to release land at Glanmor Isa for recultivation, and in June the final traces of 244s occupation disappeared with the removal of the Bessoneau hangars.

A similar fate awaited the R.N.A.S. station at Llangefni — the ariships became surplus to requirements and the men were posted to other units or released from service. But it was another two years before the Admiralty relinquished the site and allowed it to be transferred to the Government Disposal Board for sale in November 1920. An eager buyer was already waiting — Anglesey County Council — who turned the accommodation site into a small hospital, and used remaining buildings to store materials and equipment. No useful purpose could be found for the main airship shed, and so it was dismantled and sold off in small lots, mostly to local farmers.

When assessing the value of airship patrols in the anti-submarine campaign there is no doubt that they proved an effective method of keeping U-boats at bay. As Captain T.B. Williams remarked, "No ship on the sea was lost when being escorted by these airships, when travelling either in or out of convoy." Nevertheless, submarines did succeed in sinking many vessels sailing in the Irish Sea throughout the war, posing a very serious threat, but without the reassuring presence of airships, the situation would have been far worse.

The same could be said of 244 Squadron at Aber — its worth cannot be assessed through positive results, but the very fact of constant patrolling was enough of a deterrent in itself. Captain Campbell thought the aircraft a valuable asset. He wrote, "In the month of April ten ships were sunk in the Irish Sea and in the month of October when more submarines were operating, only two — both on occasions when the weather was unsuitable for aircraft."

H.A. Jones, the military historian, described coastal patrol squadrons as, "the Cinderella of the air war", which seems fair, considering the faults and deficiencies of hasty organisation, inadequate aircraft and equipment, low quality aircrew, and lack of facilities, which characterised them. Despite these shortcomings however, the squadrons, 244 included, did sterling work.

Having been in existence for a few months only, 244 Squadron had little chance to develop 'esprit de corps', but at R.N.A.S. Llangefni, in contrast, a strong feeling of camaraderie had grown amongst officers and ratings after three years. Shortly after the war an Old Boys' Association was formed, which held annual reunions until 1970, by which time so few members remained that it was resolved to make that year's meeting the last.

In 1969 Flight Lieutenant W. Shuttleworth, an ex-pilot

decided to present Anglesey County Council with a commemorative plaque, "On behalf of the Officers, Petty Officers and Ratings who served on the Airship Station during World War I." It was positioned in the main entrance to the Shire Hall, Llangefni and was to be officially unveiled on December 6th, but a few weeks before the ceremony Flt. Lt. Shuttleworth died. However, the ceremony went ahead as planned, with ten 'old boys' attending. The plaque shows an outline map of Anglesey, with SSZ34 superimposed, its trail rope hanging down and pointing to the station's location near Llangefni.

Specification of S.S.Z. airship

Volume: 70,000 cubic feet
Beam: 30 feet
Overall height: 44 feet 6 inches
Length of car: 18 feet 6 inches
Four bladed propeller; diameter 7 feet 10 inches
Fuel capacity: 102 gallons
Oil: 4½ gallons
Water ballast: 28 gallons
Engine: Rolls-Royce Hawk, 75 h.p.
Endurance: at 1,300 r.p.m. – 16 hours, speed 56 m.p.h.
        fuel consumption 6½ gallons per hour

        at 700 r.p.m. – 40 hours, speed 20 m.p.h.
        fuel consumption 2½ gallons per hour
Crew: Three
Bomb load: 130 lb.
Lift: gas at 95% purity – 4,500 lb.

De Havilland D.H.6

Primary trainer built to meet the needs of a rapidly expanding RFC. Designed with ease of manufacture and simplicity of repair as important considerations. Performance and elegance of line was sacrificed to this end. The aircraft had many nicknames, e.g. The Clutching Hand, (because of heavily cambered wings), and Sky Hook.

Dimensions: Span 35' 11"
Length 27' 3½"
Height 10' 9½"
Wing Area 436.3 square feet

Engine: One 90 h.p. RAF 1A V8 aircooled engine, (but when production outstripped that of the 1A some D.H.6s were powered by 80 h.p. Renault and 90 h.p. Curtiss OX-5 engines).

Weight: Empty 1,460 lb.
Loaded 2,000 lb.

Performance: Maximum Speed 66 m.p.h.
climb 225 feet per minute
endurance 2¾ hours

Chapter 6

AVIATION BETWEEN THE WARS
(1919-1939)

With the closure of R.N.A.S. Llangefni and the R.A.F. camp at Aber in 1919 a period of inactivity, in aviation terms, descended upon the area which lasted more or less for the decade of the 1920's. Little of any permanent significance took place with only a few isolated incidents to record such as the attempt at an Atlantic crossing that failed near Holyhead, a few accidents, publicilty flights by R.A.F. seaplanes, and the ill fated R101 airship for instance. Plans to introduce civil aviation were considered but never went beyond the discussion stage. In general it was a barren period.

Then, in the 1930's the previous decades bleakness gave way to a more interesting and enlivened period. The famous travelling air display organised by Sir Alan Cobham visited all the major towns, thus bringing aviation (albeit of the barnstorming variety) closer to most people than ever before. Private flying increased; a gliding club was formed, and strong, if ineffectual, efforts were made to promote civil aviation.

But without doubt the decade's most significant development was the establishment of military aviation, on a permanent basis, in Gwynedd. This was the R.A.F. armament training school built at Penrhos in 1936. Its construction aroused strong political opposition in Wales which culminated in a token attempt at arson by Welsh Nationalists. Penrhos's controversial beginnings are fully described at the conclusion of the chapter.

One area of growth in aviation hindered by the war was commercial flying, but when the Armistice came in November 1918, plans to organise development were introduced almost immediately. In accordance with these plans, in January 1919 Sir Frederick Sykes was appointed the first Controller General of Civil Aviation. Sykes, with a small staff and an equally small budget, worked under great pressure to complete the immense task of preparing regulations, surveying land for airfields, issuing licences etc. before May 1st — set by the government as the first day of authorised civil flying.

With the hope of profiting from this new opportunity a number of prospective companies began to formulate plans for air services. The Great Northern Aerial Co. of Liverpool, for instance, set up with the object of establishing scheduled services between Liverpool, the Isle of Man, Ireland, and coastal resorts such as Rhyl, Colwyn Bay, Llandudno, Conwy, and Holyhead. In North Wales the main source of business would be transporting holidaymakers to and from the resorts plus a Holyhead-Dublin service which might possibly provide strong competition for sea transport. Some money was spent on feasibility investigations but the scheme, like many subsequent ones, came to nothing, and no more was heard of it.

Then on April 25th the government published details of proposed U.K. air routes. No Welsh services whatsoever were to be provided — the only provision being for emergency landing grounds in North Wales along a route from Chester (Sealand) to Dublin.

This omission prompted Sir Edgar Jones, M.P. for Merthyr, to write angrily to Sykes:- "I was astonished," he wrote, "to see in the press that the air routes for civil aviation in the UK did not provide for aerodromes anywhere in the Principality of Wales.

"This is a matter of vital importance and I shall be glad

of immediate reassurance that aerodromes will be provided and that definite routes to and from South, North, and Mid Wales respectively will be immediately sanctioned..."

"I can assure you that unless an immediate assurance is forthcoming a fierce movement of national protest and resentment will spread through the whole of the Principality... Wales will not tolerate neglect in such an important matter..." An over-reaction on Sir Edgar's part perhaps, but the reason for this alleged neglect was simply that the Government had recognised that no real potential for development existed. So much of the land was hilly making if difficult to locate suitable landing sites and in addition, much of the population lived in small rural communities, particularly in North and Mid Wales. These basically unchangeable geographical and social factors imposed limitations which curtailed any hope of profitable commercial operation, however indignant the local politicians might have felt.

Replying to Sir Edgar's letter, General Seely, Under Secretary of State for Air, pointed out these rather negative factors but went on to say that the routes outlined on April 25th were purely provisional and subject to alteration. Surveys were to be carried out, particularly in North Wales with a view to locating suitable aerodromes for traffic to Ireland, the obvious place being, of course, Holyhead. The Air Ministry would only be too glad to enter into negotiations, over sites, and the possibility of linking up with some of the English routes. General Seely conlcuded that he hoped to have more information soon.

However, despite Seely's promises, nothing actually happened. Ten months after his correspondence with Sir Edgar the possibility arose, briefly, of using Conwy Morfa as a base for air services along the coast, very much like that proposed by the Great Northern Aerial Co., but as before, it remained an idea only.

For the remainder of the decade initiatives for development were sporadic.

In December 1925 Sir Sefton Brancker, the Director of Civil Aviation, suggested that a Holyhead-Dublin seaplane service should be established as part of Irish aviation's growth. No action was taken, but the idea came up again in 1929 when Sir Robert Thomas, M.P. for Anglesey, asked the Secretary of State for Air if the possibility of using Holyhead as a terminal for customs clearance of passenger traffic by flying boats between Britain and Ireland had been considered.

The response was tactfully uncommitting — yes, it had been considered but it was thought best to adopt a 'wait and see' policy, deferring any detailed investigations until the pattern of air traffic to and from the port could be more easily discerned, and what the practical needs of that traffic were likely to be. Traffic did not develop however and the scheme was not pursued any further. There remained only an attempt by Llandudno Council, also in 1929, to establish a small airfield near the town — discussed later in the chapter.

Progress throughout the decade had been non-existent, for the reasons already stated, and North Wales was as untouched by civil aviation in 1929 as it had been in 1919.

Besides the development of civil aviation, another great challenge interrupted by World War I was the non-stop crossing of the Atlantic. Like civil flying the challenge was taken up soon after the war ended. In April 1919 two R.A.F. officers, a Major Wood and Captain Wyllie, hoping to win the £10,000 *Daily Mail* prize for the crossing, decided to make their attempt by flying from East to West against the prevailing winds, thereby making things doubly difficult for themselves (all other participants intended to start from Newfoundland). The two, however, got no closer to the New World than Holyhead!

They set out from Eastchurch, Kent, on April 18th in a modified Short Shirl, to fly to their pre-determined starting point in Ireland — The Curragh, near Kildare. Wood and Wyllie named their aircraft "Shamrock" because of this Irish starting point.

Modifications made to "Shamrock" included an increased wingspan and much greater fuel capacity, giving a range, with 435 gallons, of 3,200 miles cruising at 80 m.p.h. The extra fuel was carried in a huge, elongated tank slung underneath the fuselage.

Ominously, trouble had already been experienced with the fuel transfer system during test flights, but Wood, heedless of the warning signs, was determined to make his attempt on the Atlantic crossing, regardless. He described how the adventure began — "We started off at 3.15 p.m. on Friday... our object was to make for Holyhead and use that port as our point of departure for Dublin... (they were accompanied on this flight by Les Parker, Short's test pilot, flying another Shirl)... up till now the engine had been running perfectly and everything seemed favourable. We reached Holyhead at about 7.20 p.m. I then took over the control and Wyllie gave me the course and we started across the Channel... We got to about twelve miles out to sea when the engine stopped. The throttle was open, we turned the aircraft round and headed for the shore, eventually we landed at sea about half a mile from shore." An airlock in the fuel system was the cause of trouble.

Two men, standing on the beach at Holyhead, who witnessed the aircraft ditching, quickly grabbed a small boat and rowed to the rescue. In fact the boat was so small only one extra man could be taken on board with safety. As it turned out Wood was rescued first, and was heard to mutter angrily as he got into the boat "Atlantic flight piffed"! Holyhead lifeboat soon picked up his companion and salvaged "Shamrock", which floated well, luckily. It was later returned to Short Bros.

Following this episode Captain Wood earned the nickname Atlantic Jim, which he failed to shake off for the remainder of his R.A.F. career.

Further mishaps of a similar nature occurred in 1922 to military aircraft flying to and from Ireland. On January 27th a flight of eight Bristol fighters left Baldonnell Aerodrome for R.A.F. Shotwick (later known as Sealand) as part of the demobilisation scheme brought about by political changes (the setting up of a provisional Irish government). Whilst over the Irish Sea the flight was struck by gale force winds. One aircraft became further endangered by engine trouble. The pilot managed to reach the North Wales coast and force landed near Rhos-on-Sea.

Another accident occurred a fortnight later, on February 10th, when more aircraft were being withdrawn from Ireland. An Avro 504 from Shotwick had been detailed to rendezvous with a returning squadron and escort them to the airfield. Flying along the coast at 2,000 feet the Avro's engine failed, forcing the pilot, Flying Officer Newham, to land near Gorddinog, Llanfairfechan. The aircraft hit a fence and overturned throwing the observer, LAC Searle, out of his cockpit, but neither he nor the pilot were injured.

Some four years were to elapse before the next flying accident in Gwynedd, on June 30th 1926. The aircraft involved was a Sopwith Snipe flown by Pilot Officer Bradbury, from No.5 F.T.S. Sealand, on a training flight. Over Rhos-on-Sea the Snipe's engine stopped and it immediately began to lose height. The sands of Rhos would have been ideal for a forced landing but large numbers of people on the beach ruled this out. The risk of injuring or killing someone was too great and so Pilot Officer Bradbury chose to ditch his aircraft about 300 yards from shore. The Snipe turned turtle but Bradley, after a struggle, managed to escape from his submerged cockpit, and swam 100 yards before being picked up by boat.

Strangely enough the next accident happened on exactly the same day and month, 30th June, but two years later in 1928. A Supermarine Southampton flying boat of 480 Coastal Reconnaisance Flight had taken off from Pembroke bound for Barrow, where it was to take part in anti-submarine exercises. Some miles off Bardsey, in gale force winds, the flying boat developed engine trouble and was consequently forced down into rough seas. The crew of four had to wait anxiously for some 3½ hours before being rescued, with difficulty, by a trawler. Rescue came just in time as the Southampton was on the verge of foundering. It later became a total wreck and was lost.

More comical was the visit in September 1927 of three R.A.F. flying boats (type not specified in the newspaper account but could well be Supermarine Southamptons) to Llandudno. The town council received word from the Air Ministry that the flying boats would make "a goodwill visit" (or 'public relations' in modern parlance — an exercise still carried out, incidentally, by the R.A.F.'s premier aerobatic team the Red Arrows, who visit the resort annually, during the high season), scheduled to take place on September 12th. Members of the council and their friends were to be allowed to inspect and board the aircraft. The visit was billed as a great attraction.

On the 12th, councillors, plus hundreds of onlookers, lined the promenade to await the flying boats arrival. An official welcome had been prepared but when the aircraft came into view they did not land as expected but merely flew over the crowd, made a turn, and promptly headed back in the direction they came. This left the worthy councillors somewhat confused, and apparently very angry.

An explanation was demanded from the R.A.F., but this drew no proper reply. The risk of collision during take-off was offered as an excuse, which prompted one annoyed councillor, at the next meeting, to suggest the council should "Write the Ministry and tell them that if the boats cannot rise here they are no use. They have made a fool of the whole of North Wales." Support came from another outraged member — "We had better tell the Minister of Air if his machines cannot land in Llandudno the things are no good. It made the council look fools and it should not have happened." The chairman having allowed these feelings to be vented, tactfully said that on a point of order the matter could go no further as it came under the 'questions without discussions' heading!

Although the council might have felt temporarily ill-disposed towards flying boats they were at the same time hoping to establish a small airfield in the area, primarily in order to provide air services for holidaymakers.

A number of sites were found, the majority on land belonging to the Mostyn estate. The best location from an operating viewpoint was at Dinerth, adjoining the Colwyn Bay road, thereby providing easy communication with both resorts. Robert Loraine had landed here back in 1910 on his attempted flight to Ireland and it was also the venue for the largely unsuccessful aviation meeting of July 1911, (see chapters 2 and 4). This latest scheme did not get very far because of economics conditions, i.e. potential operators would probably find it difficult to make a profit.

A year later, in 1928, the Royal Aero Club chose Llandudno as the venue for seaplane racing during the summer. Members of the Club's racing committee negotiated with the town council, hoping to use Llandudno Bay as a starting and finishing point for races along the North Wales coast. The council however, were rather wary, and possibly with memories of the previous year's episode in mind, they turned down the suggestion. Local residents were thus deprived of an opportunity to witness sea plane racing at a time when the Schneider Trophy contests were arousing great interest.

However, one man in particular was determined to bring aviation spectacle closer to most people than ever before and make a good profit at the same time — Sir Alan Cobham. His epic flights during the 1920's made him very popular with the general public, and his forceful, persuasive personality, combining love of adventure with shrewd business sense, was admirably suited to his latest scheme.

Cobham's intention was to visit towns and cities in Britain, giving air displays and encouraging the setting up of municipal aerodromes. North Wales was on his itinerary and in April 1929 he wrote to various local authorities, Bangor and Conwy for instance, explaining his ideas and seeking permission to stage a flying display. If permission was forthcoming, he went on to say, it would be helpful if councils could also indicate the location of the largest field within their boundaries. It was a clever way of getting others to do some of the preparatory work for him.

Although permission was readily given in all cases, Cobham chose to visit Rhyl only that year. On June 27th he landed in his D.H.61 Giant Moth G-AAEV, named "Youth of Britain" at Aberkinsey Farm, between Rhyl and Dyserth, to be greeted with a civic welcome. In return he made a speech outlining his ideas, e.g., increasing air-mindedness amongst the youth of Britain (hence the naming of his D.H.61 Youth of Britain) and the need for aerodromes to be sited at important centres, in this case, Rhyl.

Unfortunately, through sheer carelessness, he marred his visit somewhat by having an accident whilst taking off in the Giant Moth with members of Rhyl town council on board. Due to a sudden wind change, he had to take off in the opposite direction to that expected, but failed to check for obstacles. Without having taken this precaution Cobham did not know that across his path lay a tree trunk. Not until the aircraft's tail came up did he see it, but by then it was too late to avoid a collision. Luckily, damage was not extensive and Rhyl's civic dignitaries were unharmed, although shaken. This visit was in fact something of a "dry run" for the more elaborate shows of the 1930's.

The decade came to an end with a visit by the ill-fated R101 airship to North Wales in November 1929. This visit was part of a round Britain flight designed to combine publicity with performance trials.

Leaving its base at Cardington, Beds., on Sunday, 17th, R101 travelled up to Scotland and then flew via Glasgow and Belfast to the Isle of Man where in the early hours of

Monday morning, turning trials were successfully completed. At 7 a.m. the airship arrived in Dublin, and then crossed to Holyhead, reaching the port at 10.30 a.m. Flying low and slow, the giant airship passed over Rhosneigr (where the navigation officer, Squadron Leader E.J. Johnston's mother lived!) and Anglesey. Johnston had further connections with Anglesey as an Old Boy of R.N.A.S. Llangefni. The officer in command of R101, Major G.H. Scott, was also ex-R.N.A.S. Llangefni and indeed had been the station's first commanding officer in 1915.

Scott, in the intervening years came to be regarded as an expert on airships and was now Assistant Director of Airship Development at Cardington.

At 10.50 a.m. R101 flew over Llandudno, its low speed and height enabling thousands of people to gain an excellent view. It then followed the coast to Chester, from where it returned to Cardington. The low height could well have been due to inadequate performance rather than a desire to show the airship's lines to admiring crowds as it became clear that not enough lift was available for the intended payload. Later, R101 was cut in half and lengthened by 50ft, thereby increasing gas capacity from 5,000,000 cubic feet to 5,500,000 cubic feet.

For many people in North Wales that day it would be the first and last time they would see such a craft. Eleven months later R101 crashed at Beauvais, France, killing 48 of the 54 men on board, including Lord Thomson, Secretary of State for Air, and Sir Sefton Brancker, Director of Civil Aviation. Major Scott and Squadron Leader Johnston also lost their lives. The accident brought to an end airship construction in Britain.

The 1930s

One of the first aviation events of this decade was a week-long flying pageant at Llandudno in 1930, which turned out to be something of a failure. The resort's Attractions Committee, who put forward the idea, set the ball rolling by hiring Northern Air Lines of Manchester to organise the pageant.

Firstly, a date was set — from September 15th to the 20th — and then a flying area was created by ripping up the hedgerows of seven fields, amounting to 35 acres, near the town.

Some of aviations leading figures were due to attend, including no less a personage than the Director of Civil Aviation himself, Sir Sefton Brancker. Others included 'Bert' Hinkler, the Australian pilot, who made the first solo flight from Britain to Australia in February 1928, and Flight Lieutenant Tommy Rose, another leading pilot of the day. Two notable woman pilots present were Winifred Brown and Winifred Spooner. The former, fresh from her success as the first woman to win the King's Cup Air Race two months previously had already paid a visit to North Wales on the strength of her success, when she was hired by the *Manchester Evening News* to give exhibition flights at seaside resorts in the region. On July 23rd she flew to Rhyl to give a short display and open a new swimming pool. In later years she settled permanently in Anglesey.

Winifred Spooner was an equally energetic and competitive woman, who came second in the 1928 King's Cup. The great Amy Johnson was expected at the pageant also, but in the event, did not make an appearance.

As the week began, any hopes of seeing these pilots in action were dashed from the start by continuously bad weather. Disappointing weather conditions meant in turn that spectators were also disappointingly few. It was a similar fate to that suffered by the previous flying show held nearly twenty years before, in July 1911.

The weather improved a little on Wednesday afternoon allowing Captain Kingswell, chief pilot of Northern Air Lines, to give an aerobatic display and for an exhibition of wing walking to take place, but little else was achieved.

On Friday evening, September 19th, the monocled and genial Sir Sefton Brancker was the guest of honour at a dinner given by Llandudno council at the Imperial Hotel. During his after-dinner speech he promised all assistance in the efforts to establish an airfield at Llandudno, but Brancker was within two weeks of his death in the R101 disaster on October 5th.

As a result of the bad weather it was decided to extend the pageant for another week in the hope that conditions would improve and allow some return to be made on expenditure. But the weather, true to form, remained as fickle as always. Indeed conditions worsened as the week passed.

On Wednesday evening, a fierce gale sprang up which lasted throughout the night. Dawn on Thursday revealed that much damage had been done. Many tents and marquees were either blown down or in a state of collapse; flagging and flattened canvas lay everywhere. Deck chairs intended for spectators who did not materialise were broken and scattered all over the field. Other equipment had also been damaged or destroyed. Worst of all, an Avro Avian left out in the open was overturned and badly damaged.

Some flying did take place in spite of the bad weather with races around the Ormes for instance. But overall, the second week was adjudged as much of a failure as the first.

In 1932 Sir Alan Cobham was back in North Wales with his travelling air show. By then it had become a well organised affair, known as the National Aviation Day Tour, with visits planned to 170 towns throughout Britain, lasting from April until October. Despite the respectability given by its name the tour was essentially 'barnstorming', pure and simple.

With financial support from Lord Wakefield, a rather motley collection of aircraft were brought together for the show, including two Airspeed Ferry 10 seaters, named "Youth of Britain" II and III, finished in silver and green livery, a Tiger Moth, Comper Swift, Southern Martlet, a Lowe-Wylde glider and an Autogiro.

The first town in North Wales to be visited was Wrexham, on June 8th. Cobham chose the area of Borras, later to become the site of a World War II airfield, on the town's outskirts as a location for his show. An added attraction put on display for the occasion was Sir Henry Seagrave's car, "The Golden Arrow".

On September 1st the show was at Bangor but poor weather and a couple of accidents spoilt proceedings. Twelve aircraft left Shrewsbury in the morning, where the previous day's display had taken place, but only seven, flying in low cloud and strong winds, managed to negotiate the Welsh mountains and locate the landing field at Tynewydd Farm, just outside Bangor.

The first aircraft arrived at noon and Cobham himself landed half an hour later to be given a civic welcome. The Mayor in his speech gave Sir Alan the benefit of a few words in Welsh, "Esgynnwch, ehedwch, a disgynnwch mewn diogelwch" ("may you ascend, fly and descend in safety") — a particularly apt sentiment in the trying circumstances of the morning, and as it turned out, the afternoon also.

Following the civic welcome, a lunch was given in Sir Alan's honour by Bangor Rotary Club at the Castle Hotel. With the aircraft grounded there was no need to hurry over lunch but by early afternoon the wind moderated sufficiently for some flying. An Air Speed Ferry proceeded to give joy rides whilst the glider's pilot thought he might be able to get airborne despite the unfavourable conditions. Launching was by means of a motor-tow, but the glider failed to gain sufficient height considering the size of the field, and the tow-line had to be released, allowing a hasty descent near the edge of the field. Seconds before touching down, the glider was caught in a violent gust and overturned. Some of the ground crew rushed to help the pilot, who, after on-the-spot medical attention was taken to hospital suffering from concussion.

Then, hardly before the excitement of this accident died down, another occurred. One of the women passengers, emerging from the Ferry after a joy ride, walked into one of its still-revolving propellers. She was immediately struck unconscious and fell to the ground, her head and face covered in blood. The medical attendants, having just sent one concussed pilot to hospital, were now, within a few minutes, faced with a second emergency. The unfortunate woman was rushed to hospital, suffering from severe scalp wounds. In fact she was extremely lucky not to have suffered more serious injury or even death.

Next day the show moved to Rhyl, utilising the same site, Aberkinsey Farm, used on Cobham's previous visit in 1929.

The tour came to an end in October, and so successful had it been that a 1933 season was planned. As far as North Wales was concerned, Wrexham and Rhos were to be visited on June 13th and 16th, and Beaumaris, Pwllheli, and Rhyl on September 10th and 11th and 12th respectively, ending with Caernarfon on October 3rd. For the coming season, 22 pilots and 100 ground staff were hired. Cobham's wife took care of the London Headquarters, whilst he and his business associate D. Eskell split between themselves managerial responsibility for pilots, mechanics and other staff.

A major undertaking of this kind called for considerable organisational skills and forward planning, but one factor not taken into account was the possibility, in Wales at least, of objections to flying shows on a Sunday!

The display at Beaumaris, for instance, was due to take place on Sunday, September 10th. When the date became known it caused an immediate outcry amongst Anglesey's religious leaders. The Chapel was still a major influence in the community social life, its ministers and elders strongly opposing any secularising influences. The *North Wales Chronicle* reported that, "Feeling still runs high in religious circles in Anglesey and Caernarvonshire regarding the air display at Beaumaris on Sunday, it was felt to be a desecration of the sanctity of the Sabbath, and sure to offend the moral welfare of young people", though it is hard to imagine how a Tiger Moth doing loops and rolls could possibly offend anyone's moral welfare. A few days before the display, Beaumaris's Methodist elders met and resolved to send a strongly-worded telegram to Cobham, expressing their displeasure and requesting that the display be cancelled.

However, no notice was taken of the request, and the display went ahead as planned, with an excellent attendance as it happened. When asked about the objections, Cobham diplomatically replied that had he known sooner about the situation he would have changed the date, but the telegram had arrived too late — which was probably true, in view of the tour's tight schedule.

The Caernarfon display was held at Griffiths Crossing, a couple of miles from the historic town. It was well attended with some good flying to satisfy the crowd. Attracting a great deal of interest was the black Gipsy Moth, flown by Jim Mollison from Australia to London, in record time during 1931.

For some reason Cobham's visit to Wales during the 1934 tour were decidedly few. Only Aberystwyth and Pwllheli were on the itinerary for July, ending with Cardiff, Barry and Port Talbot in the South during September.

Things improved slightly the following year with another visit to Pwllheli, in May, a two-day stay at Llandudno in August, and Llangefni in September. By this time the National Aviation Day tours had become an established part of aviation life in Britain and Cobham reigned supreme.

A constant theme in his speeches during these tours was the necessity for municipal aerodromes to be established and many local councils were thereby stirred to action by his zeal.

For example, in mid-1935, Rhyl Town Council spearheaded a campaign to site an airport in the Kinmel

Bay area as a link between North and South Wales and the resorts of Abergele, Colwyn Bay, Llandudno and Conway. It was believed that the potentiality existed, mainly from holidaymakers, to make services feasible. A joint committee was formed by local councils to investigate the idea and make recommendations. The Committee recommended that a conference of all interested parties be convened so that the strength of support could be assessed and consideration given to the whole advisability of the project.

The conference duly met on October 24th, 1935, at Colwyn Bay. It concluded that an airport for the area was a good thing, and that it should be sited on Rhuddlan Marsh, near Abergele. This was indeed the location suggested by Cobham himself during his visits. Furthermore it was a choice not without precedent, because as early as December 1909 an attempt had been made to establish a flying school here. In order to draw up detailed proposals the conference decided to seek expert help. A further meeting took place in April 1936, when it was agreed to submit plans to the Air Ministry for its views.

Meanwhile, in Anglesey, Holyhead Town Council had actually found an operator willing to provide services if a suitable landing ground could be made available. The operator in question was Olley Air Services Ltd., recently formed by ex-Imperial Airways pilot, Gordon Olley. However, the scheme foundered because those with land suitable for use in this way refused to permit development and no further progress was possible.

Similarly, progress on the airport at Rhuddlan Marsh quietly came to a halt. Early in 1937 Llandudno Council decided, on a "go it alone" basis, to try and establish a landing ground at Penrhyn Bay, but this idea suffered the same fate as the others. The fundamental fault was that commercial potential did not match local ambition. But to return to the Cobham tours; two days, the 6th and 7th of August 1935, were spent at Llandudno before moving to

South Wales, and then returning in September to Llangefni.

Mention must be made here to one of the pilots flying for Cobham in 1935 — Idwal Jones, a local man from Dyffryn Nantlle. Coming from a slate quarrying background he avoided ending up in the quarry by joining the R.A.F., where he trained and qualified as a pilot in 1926. After leaving the Air Force he joined Cobham's National Aviation Day Tour for the 1935 season.

At the Llangefni display, on September 12th, Idwal Jones was of course very much on home ground. He gave aerobatic performances in a Tiger Moth and also flew another aircraft from the Cobham menagerie — the highly dangerous Flying Flea.

Designed by the Frenchman Henri Mignet, the Flea was aimed at amateur constructors, but although easy and cheap to build, it was unsafe. The machine had aerodynamic deficiencies, primarily interference of airflow between front and rear wings, which under certain conditions would cause a steep dive to develop from which the unfortunate pilot was powerless to recover. A number of fatalities resulted, putting an end to the Flea's career.

At the time of its display in North Wales the aircraft's shortcomings were not known and the *North Wales Chronicle,* reporting Idwal Jones's flights at Llangefni extolled its virtues wholeheartedly — "As simple to control as a baby car and as cheap to run as a motor cycle **and actually safer than either car or motor cycle**...it can be built by the amateur for £70. In France, M. Mignet has **hundreds of disciples who have built or are building Flying** Fleas...with a little commonsense, a little capital, a few tools and plenty of patience and determination they can build and fly an aeroplane of their own... They will see a demonstration of M. Mignet's famous 'parachute descent', a nearly vertical drop of 1,000 feet on to the aerodrome with the engine stopped. This is the most impressive proof of the safety of the Flying Flea." How wrong they were.

1st A/C (Military) fatal crash in Anglesey — D.H.4 A7654 on 7th November 1917 which killed Lt. Carter, the pilot.

R.N.A.S. Anglesey airship shed during World War I.

SS25 at R.N.A.S. Anglesey.

SSZ35 moored at Llandudno.

SSP1 deflating, and two others in the shed.

*R.N.A.S. Anglesey in 1915 with T. B. Williams
by SSP1 car.*

SSP6 car and crew at R.N.A.S. Anglesey.

Officers at R.N.A.S. Anglesey in 1915.

"C3" airship from Pembroke at R.N.A.S. Anglesey.

Capt. T.B. Williams piloting airship SSP6.

Hydrogen storage tanks at R.N.A.S.
Anglesey in 1915.

*A zero non-rigid airship escorting a convoy
during World War I*

A naval airship escorting a convoy.

SS25 being towed by the launch, Amethyst, to Holyhead.

The crew by an airship car at R.N.A.S. Anglesey.

WARFARE
ANCIENT AND MODERN

An airship from R.N.A.S. Anglesey over Caernarfon Castle.

Site of R. A. F landing ground on Glanmor Isa Farm , Aber, near Bangor during 1918-1919. Photo taken in 1987.

A De Havilland 6 aircraft.

An officer with 244 Squadron in 1918.

*Short shirl "Shamrock" in Holyhead harbour after salvage,
following an unsuccessful attempt at an Atlantic crossing on
April 18th, 1919.*

Official programme of Llandudno Flying Week
15-20th September, 1930

Idwal Jones and one of C.W.A. Scott's flying display aeroplanes.

Idwal Jones and Airspeed Ferry G-ACFB

Idwal Jones with the "Flying Flea"
I-ADSC

Joan Meakin demonstrating how light the "Flying Flea" was — it could be lifted by a woman.

National Aviation Display team 1932

Sir Alan Cobham's aircraft: "Youth of Britain"

Crash of Anson K6227 at Penmaenmawr,
September 17th 1937

Supermarine Southampton at Porthdinllaen,
February 1933

MONTHLY—ONE PENNY

.The Welsh
Nationalist

ORGAN OF THE WELSH NATIONALIST PARTY

Business and Editorial—Welsh Nationalist Office, Caernarvon, North Wales

| VOLUME V | OCTOBER 1936 | NUMBER 10 |

LLŶN
DEFENCE FUND OPENED

IT is now widely known that on the night of September 7th, the preliminary buildings and the stores of the proposed English aerodrome, on the outskirts of Pwllheli, were successfully destroyed with fire by three leading members of the Welsh Nationalist Party. The law forbids any comment upon their action to be published while the matter is still before the courts. Facts alone can be given. Of particular importance are two letters received by J. E. Jones, organiser of the Party, on Tuesday, September 8th. Translated, they read as follows:—

" Dear J. E. Jones,

I enclose a copy of a letter which, with an English translation that I have made, I am taking with me tonight to the police-station at Pwllheli.

I am sorry that I could not let you know beforehand of the intention which is revealed in my letter, but if I had done so, I should, without doubt, have made the Office of the Nationalist Party suspect, and endangered it. In these circumstances, Valentine and D. J., and I, have kept the whole matter secret to this moment.

But I am perfectly sure that in our attempt tonight, we are doing our bounden duty to that country for the protection, advancement, and liberation of which we have given the best of our days. Since it is necessary for some to suffer for Wales, we desired the honour of being among the first to do so.

If I am allowed to do so, I will telephone to you in the morning from the police-station at Pwllheli."

The letter is signed " Saunders Lewis."

The letter enclosed was addressed to the Chief Constable of Caernarvon.

" Sir,

We, who sign this letter, acknowledge our responsibility for the damage done to the buildings of the Bombing School this night, September 7th.

Since the proposal to establish a bombing range in Llŷn was first announced, we, and a large number of leaders of public life in Wales, have done all in our power to persuade English Government to refrain from establishing thus in Llŷn an institution that would threaten danger to all the culture and traditions of one of the most purely Welsh area in all Wales. But despite our appeals, in despite of the letters of protest sent from hundreds of religious and secular bodies throughout Wales, and despite a petition signed by thousands of the electors of Llŷn itself, begging Government to desist from this vandalism, yet English Government refused even to receive a deputation from Wales to discuss the matter. Lawful and peaceful methods have completely failed to obtain for Wales even ordinary courtesy from English Government. Therefore, in order to compel

The Welsh Nationalist Party launch their campaign against R.A.F. Penrhos.

The three who set fire to R.A.F. Penrhos in Llŷn:
D. J. Williams, Rev. Lewis Valentine, Saunders Lewis.

Commemorative plaques at Penrhos, remembering the action of
the three leaders of 1936.

Oblique aerial view of R.A.F. Penrhos 1938.

Oblique aerial view of R.A.F. Penrhos in 1938 — note biplane in lower left hand corner (probably a Hawker Hart)

Commemorative rally celebrating 50th anniversary of the Penrhos fire on 6th June, 1986

It seems that only Mr George Essex of Penrhyn Bay, **Llandudno took the** *Chronicle*'s **advice and set about** building one. Having always been interested in aviation, Mr Essex decided to gain some practical experience and build himself an aircraft. The Flea was the obvious, and cheapest, choice. It took three months to construct, and was registered G-AEGU. Power came from a 35h.p. two cylinder Anzani engine.

However, on its maiden flight from Penrhyn Bay, the Flea stalled soon after take off and crashed on to a hut. Spectators rushed to Mr Essex but he clambered from the wreckage with only a slight cut to his forehead. Although not damaged beyond repair the aircraft never flew again. Looking back, and bearing in mind the Flea's dangerous characteristics, Mr Essex remarked, "The crash was a piece of luck really, otherwise I would have probably broken my neck flying the thing!" He died in 1984 having maintained a keen interest in aviation to the end of his life.

The 1935 National Aviation Day tour was the last organised by Cobham before he sold out to Charles Scott, another well known record breaking pilot. Operating under the slogan "Flying for all — All for Flying", Scott's fleet remained more or less unchanged from previous tours. Two towns in Gwynedd were visited during 1936 — Llangefni on May 8th and Llanfairfechan on June 19th. Idwal Jones continued to fly with the show, and was described in eulogistic terms by the *North Wales Chronicle* as "The Welsh Wizard, whose feats with a Tiger Moth are probably the most spectacular exhibition of flying skill to be seen in this country." Jones was then very much a local **hero. In 1937 he gave up stunt flying and joined North** Eastern Airways but his new job was shortlived unfortunately. On May 29th the Airspeed Courier he was piloting crashed at Doncaster killing him and three passengers.

In addition to the Charles Scott tour, a second air show toured North Wales during the summer of 1936. Known as British Empire Air Displays, it was organised by Tom

Campbell Black, a co-pilot of Scott in the 1934 MackRobertson race from England to Australia. Towns visited were Holyhead, Caernarfon and Llandudno, on July 28th, 29th, and 30th respectively. This was part of an ambitious programme, based on the Cobham tours, to visit 160 towns in as many days. Working for Black were twelve pilots, including Jack Baron and R. Doig. Unusually, the show had a female chief mechanic, Dorothy Spicer.

Everything went well, particularly at Holyhead, where perfect weather attracted a huge crowd to the display. The show at Llandudno was, as it turned out, the last of this kind of 'barnstorming' air display seen in North Wales. Campbell Black was killed two months later in a taxying accident at Speke Aerodrome.

Turning to accidents in Gwynedd during this period, besides those already mentioned three are worthy of mention.

The first involved two Supermarine Southamptons (S1230 and S1235) flying from Stranraer to their Calshot base on February 24th 1933. Approaching the North Wales coast they ran into one of the worst snow storms of that winter. Despite the snow and gale force winds they continued for a time, but eventually, over Caernarfon Bay, conditions became so bad that the Southamptons were forced to seek immediate refuge. Both machines managed to land safely in Porthdinllaen harbour. However, any impression that a safe haven had been found was quickly dispelled as the storm intensified, threatening to break the flying boats' moorings and sweep them out to sea. To prevent this happening the decision was taken to beach the boats with help from the Porthdinllaen lifeboat crew, who willingly gave all possible assistance. Beaching was valiantly carried out in the teeth of the gale, but such was its force that both machines were damaged in the process, particularly S1230. It ended up lying partly on top of a hut with its starboard side submerged.

When the storm eventually subsided, whole areas of North Wales had been isolated as enormous snow drifts blocked roads and cut communications.

Later in the year a more tragic accident occurred at Barmouth when a young female pilot killed one of her friends in an ill-considered act of very low flying. On August 30th Doreen Tyzack was giving a flying display in her Gipsy Moth G-AAGS over the Mawddach estuary as **part of the Barmouth regatta celebrations. She flew** towards the Fairbourne sandbanks where a group of her friends stood, watching. The aircraft, losing height rapidly, made directly for them and then, at the very last moment, commenced a steeply banked turn to port which Miss Tyzack misjudged.

Two men in the group were struck by the Moth's wingtip; one was killed instantly and the other, miraculously, suffered a broken arm only. The aircraft then hit the ground, bounced, and crashed in the Mawddach. A number of boats went to the rescue and found Miss Tyzack suffering from head injuries and severe shock. The two victims were brothers, Wilfred and Clifford, sons of Dr. Allport, an eye specialist from Birmingham, on holiday at Barmouth. Wilfred had little chance of survival as the aircraft's wing struck his head, and Clifford was very lucky indeed to escape with only a broken arm.

The inquest, delayed in order to allow Miss Tyzack to recover from deep and prolonged shock, recorded a verdict of accidental death due to an error of judgement on the pilot's part.

Not so apparent was the cause of an accident which killed local pilot W. P. Evans of Broom Hall, Pwllheli, in April 1937. Evans, a wealthy landowner, was one of the first private pilots in Gwynedd, flying a Puss Moth (G-AAXW) from his own airfield on his estate at Broom Hall.

On Tuesday April 9th, intending to make a flight to Surrey, he took off in the Moth but the aircraft failed to gain height, and struck a wall on the airfield boundary. It then crashed into the adjoining field. At work in this field was a rabbit catcher, Thomas Ellis, who witnessed the crash at close range. Seeing the aircraft coming towards him, he said, "I ducked as it reached the wall, and the next second heard a tearing crash. The nose of the plane seemed to rise momentarily almost alongside me and then dived into the field." He ran to the wreckage, tore open a door and dragged Evans out. He was badly injured and died a few minutes later.

At the inquest no reason for the crash could be discovered. An Air Ministry inspector had examined the Moth's wreckage but could find nothing to indicate technical failure. Neither was the aircraft overloaded, in fact it was 200lbs below the limit. One possible explanation was that Evans had ascertained wind direction somewhat crudely by holding up his handkerchief, and had then proceeded to take off downwind but the evidence was inconclusive. Certainly the area lost one of its chief protagonists of private flying.

Some years previously, in 1934, Evans was responsible, together with a small group of enthusiasts, for introducing the sport of gliding to Gwynedd. In November of that year the group met in Pwllheli and agreed to form the Pwllheli and District Gliding Club which as time passed proved to be something of a failure, unfortunately. Its history is disjointed with many annoying gaps but enough details exist to provide some idea at least of the club's activities.

The secretary, E. R. Wilson wrote to *"The Sailplane"* — "A gliding club has been formed in the district and we have 18 members to date (November 27th)... we hope to commence flying in January. Our president Lt. Evans, Broomhall, has offered us the use of his aerodrome for primary training by auto-towing and we have also had permission to use Black Rock Sands — about two miles of firm sand. A German glider pilot has offered to assist us and we have three power pilots in the club. As we are west of the Snowdon range we are hoping that the district will prove ideal for soaring, if and when we get to that stage. We are negotiating for a Dickson glider (from South Shields) which is complete except for the fabric. If successful we may have two machines."

However, the Dickson did not arrive until April 1935, forcing the club meantime to concentrate excessively on theory. It was a state of affairs which did little to maintain interest amongst members. Slowly over the months enthusiasm waned, and membership dropped.

In March Wilson wrote again to *The Sailplane* **admitting** that, "The response in forming a gliding club has been disappointing, but we are hoping that members will roll up when they see that we mean business."

The first flight was planned for Easter and according to the *North Wales Chronicle*, "Twelve members (down from the original 18) are anxiously awaiting Easter Monday when they hope to put into practice the theory which they have been absorbing in recent months." The club's president W. Evans of Broom Hall had placed his private airfield at their disposal, and from this location the first flight duly took place.

Wilson's next dispatch to the *Sailplane* reveals a rather inauspicious start to flying... "On Easter Monday we had our first meeting when the secretary (Wilson himself) just managed to leave the ground. The car used was under-powered and not a breath of wind to help... We have disposed of the incomplete Dickson and have purchased another primary with detached nacelle, with which we are very pleased (no indication of type however). Our winch car is not yet ready."

"On Thursday April 25th we met again. There was a strong gusty wind and on the first tow the poor secretary was kited above the trees, but made a safe landing. Several members had ground slides, and later, after the wind had dropped, three were safely launched on their first hops. One lost his foothold and the stick, hanging over the side by the belt, but the machine brought him down safely. It served to bring home the lesson that the machine will fly itself!"

Thereafter meetings took place each week until May 16th when a new, more powerful launching car was put to use, and also the first bad accident occurred, severely damaging the club's sole machine.

One of the female members, a Miss Fowden Jones, stalled the glider at a height of twenty feet. The aircraft crashed on to its starboard wing, the nose broke off, and then it started to overturn, coming to rest on the port wing leading edge. Finally the tail snapped. Miss Fowden Jones received bad cuts to her leg. This accident put an end to flying for the next two months — the time taken by members to carry out repairs. By August the glider was airworthy again.

Wilson reported the towing car was doing its job satisfactorily and that several hops of 40-50 feet were completed. This seems to have been the club's sole achievement up to that point, nobody apparently having flown a circuit or a flight of any length. The record for September continues as follows:—

"September 5th — Few members present and the wind still up the slope (no indication of the location but obviously not Broom Hall as there is mention of a slope) but we reached about 100 feet and commenced practising turns. Mr Darbishire our vice-president, Wilson and Davies had hops.

September 12th — Several hops in the afternoon. After tea on the first flight Wilson had an argument with a wall. After a good climb he commenced a circuit to the left, found the trees too near to be healthy and turned back into wind, only to find himself landing towards a stone wall — running at an angle of 45° to the wind, from left to right. He touched down a few yards from the wall and then endeavoured to pivot away on the starboard wing, the port wing skimmed over the wall and caught in the barbed wire carrying away the flying wire bracket and four ribs.

Mercifully she stopped before the nose made contact with the wall.

September 17th — Repairs once again completed."

This is the last report of the club's activities. Probably gliding continued but it is not known in what form and with what frequency.

Wilson's name does however crop up again in print when *The Times* for January 10th 1938 reported another gliding accident in which he was involved. "E. R. Wilson of Abersoch, a member of the Midland Gliding Club was saved by a wall from crashing over a cliff while gliding at Llanbedrog Head yesterday. At a height of 20 feet in a strong wind the machine dived and crashed into the wall only a few feet from the cliff edge. Wilson escaped almost uninjured."

There are unconfirmed reports that gliding continued right up until the summer of 1939 at Pwllheli, but overshadowing all else, in aviation matters, during the latter half of the 1930's was a much more important and significant development — the coming of military aviation to Gwynedd as a result of R.A.F. expansion schemes. The first signs of what lay ahead came in August 1935 when Beaumaris town council asked Anglesey's MP, Megan Lloyd George, if she could persuade the Air Ministry to establish an airfield in the area. This would obviously be good for local employment and trade, in the council's view. Megan Lloyd George carried out the request but the Air Ministry was not encouraging. They promised a survey of the island to locate a possible site for a flying training school but it would take time, and furthermore the Ministry thought the number of potential sites in Anglesey very limited. This greatly pleased Beaumaris's leading resident, Sir Richard Williams-Bulkeley, owner of the huge Baron Hill estate, judging by the strongly worded attack he made on the council for putting forward the idea of a local airfield — "This I would oppose to the best of my ability," he said, "unless it were conclusively shown that the strategical importance of the position was such as to over-ride all other considerations."

"Do the people of Beaumaris realise that it would be an invitation to the enemy to bomb the district generally and the aerodrome in particular?"

"If the strategic situation was of sufficient importance we must take the risk of course but that would be decided by the military authorities," he continued, "but to ask for it in the hope of making a little money out of it does seem to me to be not distantly related to war profiteering." Clearly Sir Richard did not want his peace and quiet disturbed.

He need not have worried unduly because at this particular time the Air Ministry was not interested in Anglesey, but it was very interested in a small corner of the Llŷn Peninsula, a few miles from the town of Pwllheli. Here the ministry proposed to build an armament training airfield for the R.A.F. As the reader will no doubt be aware, in order to fulfil its expansion plans the R.A.F. needed a number of training airfields, where newly recruited aircrew could be taught the techniques of bombing, air gunnery etc.

Initially, sites in England were explored, Lydd, Chesil Bank and Holy Island for example, but in each case fierce local opposition thwarted plans. Finally, after an exhaustive survey the Air Ministry decided, in May 1935, on the site in Gwynedd.

It was in a quiet, unspoilt part of Llyn, which, despite its rural picturesqueness contained much poverty and therefore, as in the case of Beaumaris, prospects of improved employment opportunities aroused much local support for the project.

On the other hand, general reaction in Wales was far more guarded, and in the case of the Welsh Nationalist party, extremely hostile. Indeed, the Nationalists had maintained strongly pacifist attitudes throughout the 1930s in the face of re-armament and military expansion schemes. Once they learnt of the plans for Llyn they quickly mounted a vigorous campaign against the airfield.

organising public meetings, petitions, and lobbying M.P.s, all to no avail. In June 1936 the party leaders, frustrated by their lack of progress, decided to take their case to the **Prime Minister himself, Stanley Baldwin.**

He was asked to receive a deputation of protestors but the request was adamantly refused in a letter which went on to say that the Air Ministry had already carried out an exhaustive search of the U.K. pinpointing only eight areas which fulfilled the requirements for an armament training school — viz.

   a)   a large sea area reasonably free from shipping
   b)   good weather conditions
   c)   unobstructed approaches to the targets from a landward site
   d)   good airfield site in the vicinity

Furthermore the Prime Minister added, land had been purchased and construction started. In the circumstances there seemed little purpose in receiving a deputation. This **reaction caused great anger amongst the Nationalists, who saw the decision as being grossly unfair, bearing in mind that similar deputations had been received from English** protestors. They resolved to continue the fight by every means.

Meanwhile, as Baldwin said, the plan was already underway. Over two hundred acres of land had been purchased at Penrhos, just outside Pwllheli, plus land at **Hell's Mouth, (Porth Neigwl, in Welsh), a wide bay some six miles to the south west. Levelling was being carried out** whilst the Nationalists still protested. A bombing range **was to be established at Hell's Mouth and the associated** airfield at Penrhos.

By September 1936 large quantities of building material had been deposited by various contractors at Penrhos. With construction work about to begin the Nationalists **were forced to concede defeat, their protest having failed** to make even the slightest dent in government resolve, a fact which left them feeling bitter and frustrated. The only gain seemed to be a great deal of publicity for the Nationalist movement in Wales but it was not sufficient in any way to overcome the sense of disappointment felt by party members over their failure.

In addition, the fact that these events took place when they did had a special significance for the party because the **year 1936 saw the 400th anniversary of the Act of Union** 1536 by which Wales was assimilated into the English system of government. So strong was feeling over Penrhos and the government's behaviour that it was decided to commit a final act of defiance by starting a fire at the new airfield. This was to be a token act however and not a serious attempt at arson.

Building material, most of which was timber and contractor's huts, also wooden, were to be the targets. **Three leading members were chosen to do the actual burning — Saunders Lewis, an ascetic looking intellectual from Swansea University, Lewis Valentine, a minister of** religion, and D. J. Williams, an amiable, kindly schoolmaster from Fishguard, (who forgot his matches) — never was there such an unlikely trio of arsonists.

In the early hours of Tuesday 8th September 1936 they set alight a quantity of timber and huts at Penrhos as planned, making sure that no risk to life arose from this act. Then they calmly drove to Pwllheli police station and gave themselves up to a very surprised policeman.

Their subsequent treatment aroused as much controversy as the initial protest in the first place. At the trial held in Caernarfon during October a Welsh jury failed to agree on a verdict, because of the circumstances of the crime. A retrial was expected in January 1937 but to everyone's surprise the trial was transferred to the Old Bailey as legal authority argued that a fair trial was impossible in Wales. Conversely, some people argued that a fair trial in England was impossible, and that taking the case to London was a tacit admission the government felt no jury in Wales was prepared to convict.

An Old Bailey jury had no difficulty in finding Lewis,

Valentine and Williams guilty of arson and malicious damage. They were given a prison sentence of nine months, which to be fair, did not seem excessively heavy, appearing indeed to recognise that strongly held political beliefs rather than purely criminal motivations caused the three to act as they did. Within Welsh Nationalist circles the episode has become a legend, which still stirs the party faithful.

Fifty years after the event, on September 6th 1986, a rally was held by the Nationalists at Penrhos during which a fairly elaborate three panelled plaque, costing over £2,000, was unveiled to commemorate the burning. It is to be found a quarter of a mile from the main road by the entrance to the caravan park which now takes up most of the airfield. There can be no other wartime airfield surely which boasts a memorial plaque to those that tried to burn it down!

But to return to the story of Penrhos in 1937, work continued apace with extra security in case of another Nationalist attack. The new grass field was circular and raised to a height of about twenty feet above the surrounding, rather marshy, land especially on the southern side of the airfield — an obvious hazard which caused many accidents during World War II. All hangars, workshops and other buildings were at the northern end in the lee of some small hillocks. At Hell's Mouth targets were buoyed out to sea and a small airfield cum range prepared adjacent to the beach.

In February the Air Ministry announced that Penrhos would open as No.5 Armament Training Camp on March 1st, St. David's Day, a singularly inappropriate, almost provocative choice it seemed in the light of recent events! It was, of course, an oversight and the date was quickly changed to March 20th.

There was to be no actual opening ceremony, of this, Gwynedd's first purpose built airfield, in case of further disruption. Key personnel had already arrived in February, including the Commanding Officer, Wing

Commander T. Lister. Six Westland Wallaces, obsolete as day bombers and relegated to target towing duties, were to operate in this capacity at Penrhos, plus a marine section, consisting of five Range Patrol Boats, based in Pwllheli harbour, whose job it was to look after targets sited at sea. The intention was that various training squadrons would be sent on short detachments of a month or so to the airfield.

Unfortunately bad weather and gales delayed the start of training by sweeping away targets and buoys at Hell's Mouth. Their re-setting was further hampered by continuing strong winds and high seas. Eventually everything was ready for Course No.1, a group of 34 aircraft from No.10 FTS (Flying Training School), Tern Hill, who flew into Penrhos in mass formation on Aril 3rd.

Soon the new station settled down to its daily routine of aerial gunnery and bombing practice as various units, mostly from Flying Training Schools came and went on their training courses. In the background, however, was the fear, greatly exaggerated in fact, of another attack by Welsh Nationalists. The burning of materials and huts had been a single symbolic gesture but it created a feeling of distrust and fear which lasted a long time at Penrhos.

Not unexpectedly, with so many training squadrons using the airfield flying accidents became far more commonplace than hitherto. The first occurred within weeks of the station's opening, when, on April 23rd, an Avro Tutor from 6FTS, Netheravon, crashed on the sands near Gwyllt Headland, Portmadoc, whilst attempting a practice forced landing. The trainee pilot was trapped in his cockpit and could not be rescued before the machine caught fire, but his observer escaped from the rear cockpit with minor injuries only.

Another aircraft, Audax K7350, this time from No.2 FTS, R.A.F. Digby flew into cloud covered Garn Fadryn, a 1,200 foot high hill about seven miles north east of Penrhos on August 6th 1937. The two occupants had a lucky escape, suffering nothing worse than slight injuries and shock. Few survive this type of accident, and it seems probable that last minute avoiding action was successfully taken.

Some weeks later, on September 17th, fourteen Ansons of 220 Squadron, R.A.F. Bircham Newton, Norfolk, left Penrhos for their base, having completed training. The first leg of their journey was a flight along the North Wales coast to Sealand. Soon after becoming airborne one aircraft developed engine trouble and returned to Penrhos. It made a forced landing but in doing so hit a stationary aircraft, damaging both machines.

Meanwhile the remainder, now an unlucky thirteen, continued along the coast at 2,000 feet in worsening weather conditions. Increasing amounts of low cloud obscured the coastline and hills of North Wales. When the formation reached Penmaenmawr Mountain, most of which was hidden by cloud, the leader indicated by hand signal a climb to 3,000 feet. All climbed safely to this height except one pilot who maintained a dangerously low altitude. It seems that he missed the leader's signal and, wishing to remain in visual contact with the ground, was forced ever downwards by a lowering cloud base.

As the ill fated Anson, (K6227), approached Penmaenbach, an 800 foot high headland on the coast between Penmaenmawr and Conwy, it was seen by workers on the nearby railway line, who estimated its height at only 300 feet.

The pilot did not see the obstruction until the last minute and pulled his aircraft into a steep climbing turn to port, but in the turn flying speed was lost and the Anson stalled. It went into a dive, plunging into the sea 200 yards from shore, killing the three men on board.

Another Anson became lost in cloud shortly after passing over Penmaenmawr. It flew up the Conwy valley but the pilot soon realised his mistake and returned to the coast, passing over the scene of the recent crash before regaining the correct course. Rescuers mistakenly assumed this Anson was searching for the crashed one.

The pilot knew nothing of his colleague's death until he landed at Sealand.

At the inquest on the dead airmen the jury expressed their concern over safety matters — "it is hoped that in areas like this every possible attention is given to weather reports. We, like many other people are alarmed at the increase in RAF tragedies in recent months... We feel that a reference to this sort of thing will bring all pilots to realise the conditions existing in areas like this."

But the next accident occurred in roughly similar circumstances just two months later. On November 29th a squadron of twenty aircraft, Hawker Harts and Audaxes, from No.2 FTS, Brize Norton, in Oxfordshire, were to take off for Penrhos. After eighteen had departed, a telephone message from Penrhos stated that the weather in North Wales had deteriorated to extensive fog and rain. One aircraft returned to base but the others continued with the first leg of their journey, to R.A.F. Sealand, where another ten landed. Seven flew on towards Penrhos, by then hidden by banks of fog from Pwllheli to Caernarfon. Only four succeeded in locating the airfield and landing safely. The other three aircraft, one Hart and two Audaxes, crashed at various points.

The Hart came down at Penygroes, about fifteen miles from the airfield, injuring the two occupants, but not seriously. One Audax crashed at Efailnewydd, three miles from Penrhos. Luckily the pilot and his passenger were unhurt. The pilot of the other Audax narrowly avoided crashing in the middle of Pwllheli itself, and eventually made a forced landing in an all too small field near the village of Llannor. The aircraft hit a wall, killing the pilot and seriously injuring his observer.

At the subsequent court of inquiry some criticism was made of weather forecasting and reporting facilities at Penrhos, and a recommendation made that a qualified meteorologist be employed. However, a year was to pass before the suggestion became reality and a Meteorological

Office was opened, on February 1st 1939, with a staff of two.

On June 1st 1938, Penrhos provided refuge for Aer Lingus' DH86 "Eire", caught in a storm whilst flying the daily scheduled service from Croydon via Bristol to Dublin. With nine passengers on board, including the Lord Lieutenant of Oxfordshire, the aircraft was at 6,000 feet over Barmouth, battling through the bad weather when it was struck by lightning, putting the radio and compass out of action. By flying very low, more or less hugging the coastline, the DH86 pilot located Penrhos and made a hazardous but successful landing in strong winds and torrential rain.

The worst accident of 1938 came in October when two Ansons collided near Pwllheli killing three men and injuring another.

On a brighter note, the year's highlight, certainly for local residents, was Empire Air Day on May 28th when Penrhos was thrown open to the public. Over 10,000 people turned up — a totally unexpected number for which the R.A.F. was unprepared. As many came in cars, "some disorganisation of traffic was experienced" in the words of the local paper. It was probably the first traffic jam in Llŷn. The proceeds from the Open Day amounted to £425, which was donated to the Air League of the British Empire.

During the afternoon a flying display was put on by the resident Wallaces, plus Hawker Furies and Audaxes, on detachment for training.

Outside the airfield, bands of Welsh Nationalists enthusiastically handed out anti-militarist leaflets and stuck large posters to trees, telegraph posts and gate-posts. For this act, twelve Nationalists, including the Party Secretary, found themselves in front of the local magistrates, charged somewhat quaintly "with disfiguring the natural beauty of the landscape". Fining the Secretary £1 and eleven other defendants 5 shillings (25 pence), the

Bench Chairman said he hoped this would be the last echo of their protest against Penrhos.

At this time, the Party's pacifist arguments were rapidly becoming unrealistic as events in Germany made it increasingly clear that another European war was a real possibility, if not a certainty.

By 1939 Penrhos had become very active with an ever increasing number of volunteer pilots and aircrew arriving for armament training. Even week ends were now being used, Sundays included. This led the local community, for whom Sunday was normally sacrosanct to complain in no uncertain manner. Some discontent had already been expressed at low flying and noise, but to disturb the Sabbath was unpardonable.

So seriously was the question taken that in June a meeting took place between the Air Minister — Sir Kingsley Wood, Caernarfonshire M.P. Major G. Owen, Lloyd George, representatives of religious denominations, and local authorities in the area. After what was diplomatically described as "a frank discussion" the outcome was not unexpected given the pressure to prepare for war — weekend training would continue.

In the spring of 1939 Penrhos had another open day, on **Empire Air Day — Saturday May 20th. Again the R.A.F.** had a surprise when only 5,000 people attended, a 50% reduction over the previous year. Possibly the explanation lay in the Welsh Nationalist campaign against Penrhos. Given a chance to visit the airfield which had caused so much controversy in Wales, people did so in large numbers, but once their curiosity was satisfied they had no further interest.

Those that did visit Penrhos saw an improved display from that of 1938, both on the ground and in the air. Amongst the aircraft types to be seen were the Wallace, Avro Tutor, Magister, Audax, Gloster Gauntlet, Fairey Battle and Handley Page Hampden. An Airspeed Oxford was also due to take part in a mass fly-past but some thoughtless spectator put his foot through the wing fabric!

However, this would be the last air show in Gwynedd for some time. As the months of 1939 passed it was not too difficult to discern that another European war was imminent. It became a reality on September 1st when German forces invaded Poland. Two days later Britain declared war on Germany.

There is a brief but interesting account in print given by Richard Passmore in his book "Blenheim Boy" (Thomas Harmsworth Publishing, London 1981) of life in camp at Penrhos during this momentous period. Passmore was a **WOP/AG, (wireless operator/air gunner), with a squadron of Blenheims at the time and wrote of his experience...** "Then it was August 14th and we were off to Penrhos for the annual practice camp. We would live in tents, act as a detached squadron in the field, without any permanent buildings, and generally play at boy scouts for fourteen glorious days. There was an infectious holiday atmosphere. We worked to the same high standards but with a kind of informality. The food was decidly unusual, being cooked in World War I field cookers. The usual Offices were primitive. But the weather was glorious: we spent every day in the open air, taking-off for short flips to fire our guns or drop bombs on the nearby range, appropriately called Hell's Mouth. We raided the orchard on the gentle slope of the hill behind the camp, feeling like guilty schoolboys. For entertainment we lay of an evening on top of the cliff at Glyn-y-Weddw, watching the courting couples below, or scrounged lifts on one of the trucks going into Pwllheli.

The impending war was creeping up on us quite quickly now and we realised that it might be on us even before our camp was over..."

..."That evening (August 30th) there was a monumental flap. We were instructed to break off camp and return to base the following morning; war was imminent."

A week after war had been declared Penrhos was designated No.9 Air Observers School and equipped with Harrows and Battles. On November 1st after another change of name the school became No.9 Bombing and Gunnery School.

Until then Penrhos was Gwynedd's only airfield, but the war soon brought a series of others, in an unparalleled period of development. The region's under utilisation, in aviation terms, was well and truly over.